Healing Into
Immortality

Healing Into Immortality

A New Spiritual Medicine of Healing Stories and Imagery

Gerald Epstein, M.D.

BANTAM BOOKS
NEW YORK • TORONTO • LONDON • SYDNEY • AUCKLAND

This book is not intended as a substitute for medical advice of physicians. The reader can consult a physician in matters relating to his or her health and particularly in respect to any symptoms that may require diagnosis or medical attention.

HEALING INTO IMMORTALITY
A Bantam Book / December 1994

Library of Congress Cataloging-in-Publication Data

Epstein, Gerald, 1935–
    Healing into immortality : a new spiritual medicine of healing stories and imagery / Gerald Epstein.
        p.   cm.
    Includes index.
    ISBN 0–553–35191–5
    1. Mental Healing.   2. Mind and body.   I. Title.
RZ400.E67   1994
615.8'52—dc20   94–17700
                                                                    CIP

Published simultaneously in the United States and Canada

PRINTED IN THE UNITED STATES OF AMERICA

BVG   0 9 8 7 6 5 4 3

For Colette—my luminous guide and teacher,
without whom this book could not have been written

Contents

Acknowledgments

———————

I must acknowledge at the outset all of those teachers whom I've had the good fortune to meet in this lifetime who have contributed to my evolution. I am doing so not because I consider this book to be my last one but because I consider it to be my magnum opus, the culmination to date of my lifetime of study and experience as a medical doctor and as a seeker after spirit.

With this book I believe I am fulfilling this life's mission, which has been to share with as many people as possible, both near and far, through personal contact and these writings, ways to make a healing turn in their lives and put themselves on a path toward spirit and in making union with God. I have written all of my previous books and articles as a medically trained man who has provided medical (that is, healing) ways for people to become well and self-reliant. I have not previously sought to put a spiritual stamp on my output because the context did not necessarily call for it.

In this book, I am again writing from the perspective of a doctor, but now I am providing ways of healing that have cosmic implications. Because of the importance I attach to the subject matter of this book, I must give credit to those who have helped me along the way. I shall list them in the order they entered my life.

Max and Celia Epstein, my parents, who gave me the opportunity to enter this earth and discover what I have come to know. This book is a tribute to their blessed memory.

Allen Koenigsberg, who entered my life when I was twelve years old and directed my attention to the presence and truth of extrasensory perception, parapsychology, and the notion of following the beat of your own drummer.

Perle Besserman, who, as my first wife, directed my perception to the presence and truth of the life of spirit and its supreme importance in our lives. She is the most serious and sincere seeker I have ever known.

Sybil Ferguson, perhaps the greatest psychic of this age and considered by some to be the most important spiritual being alive while on this earth. She always encouraged me and was a great support. Her memory is revered.

Colette Aboulker-Muscat, who has been the most significant influence in my life. It is her teaching, screened through my filter, that inspired all the books I have written. It is through her that I found my true spiritual path. She has been the example of the love that one human being can have not only for this one fortunate soul, but for all humanity. It is to her that this book is dedicated.

Philo of Alexandria, the enlightened Hellenistic Jewish philosopher who helped me, through his writings, plumb the depths of the spiritual Judaism that is at the heart of the Old Testament. I never tire of reading him and being filled.

Medard Boss, the recently deceased Swiss psychiatrist, who provided a meaningful context for understanding human beings through both his person and his writings. I treasure my all too brief relationship with him.

Valentin Tomberg, who as the "Unknown Friend" wrote the book *Meditations on the Tarot,* a beacon of eternal light that has come to us as a gift of love. This book was made known to me by a man in a bookshop who told me to buy it. I am convinced this man was an angel who bestowed grace on me. This "living" dead teacher guided me through the most stormy and life-threatening period of my existence.

Bob Gibson, a former physician who has provided one of the simplest, clearest, and most powerful spiritual practice guides imaginable. It is said that he received his transmission from an angel. His work is truly heaven sent.

To my wife, Rachel, who besides organizing the content and flow of this book, has shown me what it means to receive love, to allow nourishment. She has brought a great gift to me in this lifetime.

I would like to give a nod to some people who have been there to help and share over the years, particularly when I needed it: Sheikh Musaffer, Jim Tumelty, Barry Flint, Mark Seem, Ingo Swann, Jerome Rainville, Harry Palmer, Tobi Sanders, Harris Dientsfrey, the writings of Ceanne DeRohan, Mary Montgomery, Mary Elizabeth Avicenna, and Anita Eshay. For all of these personages I have felt, and for some I still feel, deep love and gratitude. I can only hope that whatever I produce does justice to their efforts on my behalf.

I must also acknowledge Caroline Shookhoff for yet another masterful job of helping to prepare the manuscript, for her ability to read my handwriting and make coherent sense out of it.

Acknowledgment is due here to Manuela Soares,

whose editorial skills were instrumental in organizing the mass of information in this book.

A debt of thanks goes to Janet Thormann-Mackintosh, who helped me in the final editing of the book in a masterful way.

Finally, my appreciation goes to Leslie Meredith, my editor at Bantam Books, who has persevered in keeping up with my ideas about the spiritual dimension of healing and has contributed significantly to my own understanding.

And, lastly, a tip of the hat to Janet Biehl, an extraordinary copyeditor who did a masterful job of helping to polish the manuscript.

Preface

In 1974, I was sitting in the garden of my teacher Colette Aboulker-Muscat on a beautiful June day in Jerusalem, at the beginning of what was to be a nine-year apprenticeship in Western spiritual medicine. I had just finished some mental imagery that had taken me to levels of reality where I had met my inner guide. I was now sharing a cup of spearmint tea and honey cake and enjoying the wonderful aroma of jasmine from the tree in her garden. A thin bespectacled man whom neither of us knew came strolling by. He peered into the garden and, seeing us in that idyllic setting, boomed out in a deep stentorian voice: *"It reminds me of the days of the prophecies,"* whereupon he strolled away. I did not see this man again until January 1986, when I was in the Paraclete Bookshop in New York City.

The Paraclete is a bookstore with a full assortment of religious and spiritual books of all persuasions. In January 1986, I was there looking for books on mental imagery. A number of them were written from religious perspectives, including manuals of therapeutic imagery written during the Middle Ages and the Renaissance by Saint Ignatius and Saint Hildegard of Bingen. I collected about six books and lined them up on a table in preparation for paying for them. There were one or two other people in line ahead of me waiting to pay. Suddenly, a thin bespectacled man in a trench coat with an upturned collar and a five o'clock shadow brushed by me, picked up and riffled through each one of the books, then slammed each down on the table with obvious disgust. He then walked off, and as he did so, he turned toward me, pointed to a book on a table near him, and said that I should buy this book. I looked down to see the book he was pointing to. It was *Meditations on the Tarot*. I felt at once puzzled and skeptical. Although I hesitated, haltingly I lifted it. As I flipped through its pages, I came across diagrams (I'm a sucker for diagrams) that leaped out at me from the pages, diagrams in the form of the Star of David and the Tree of Life as well as the Greek Cross and other such religio-spiritual drawings. I felt excited, so I decided to buy this book and forgo the others. I went to the front door where the man had just exited to thank him. When I got outside, he was nowhere to be seen.

On reflection, I realized that I had been visited on these two occasions, in Jerusalem and in New York, by an angel, as Abraham had been nearly 3,900 years ago. The two encounters were pivotal events for me, pointing me in a new direction and forever changing my life. At least I like to think of this man as an angel, for that is really how I experienced him. *Meditations on the Tarot* has since become instrumental in my thinking and in my understanding of health and disease. The writer—who calls himself "Unknown Friend"—seems to be speaking to me directly with endless wisdom and inspiration.

My life has been truly blessed in terms of the unusual people of a psychic and spiritual nature who have entered my life and influenced my thinking and personal development. I have met swamis, lamas, Zen masters, Sufi masters, Kabbalistic rabbis, renowned psychics, and healers of many persuasions, culminating in my relationship and work with Colette. It surely has been an eventful and fruitful journey to this point, one that has shaped my life's direction and led to this book.

Introduction

———————

Healing Into Immortality represents a homecoming, a coming home to the Western perspective on spirit and healing. In the latter half of this twentieth century, many seekers have turned to the East for spiritual sustenance and healing guidance. Many of us had yearned for an understanding of the deeper, esoteric realities and spiritual wisdom that we could not seem to find in the institutional religions of the West—in Judaism, Christianity, or Islam. For a time, the East had helped us fill this void. I was fortunate, however, to discover the Western esoteric tradition through the good graces of my teacher, Colette Aboulker-Muscat. I believe that, as Westerners, we are born into this Western tradition not by chance but for the purpose of using it to find our own way to spiritual wholeness and health. I am a practicing physician, so I channeled my discoveries into my practice of medicine, hoping to reestablish the links to ancient attitudes and ancient traditions of wisdom.

In this book, I provide a basic guide to uniting the spirit and the bodymind to heal ourselves of various illnesses and of attitudes detrimental to health, and to maintain wellness. I discuss stories from our Western religious tradition that tell us what we must do and that show the ways we should act to promote health, well-being, and harmony in ourselves and in the people around us. I supply a number of effective techniques for healing, including seven keys to healing and numerous imagery exercises that are salubrious bridges between the spirit and the bodymind.

You need not be a Westerner to benefit from these methods and teachings, just as you need not be an Easterner to benefit from Eastern traditions of wisdom. But if you are a Westerner, you may find your whole being resonating to this new—or rather, reclaimed—vision of the full meaning of health and healthy spirituality.

This book presents the results of my nearly thirty years of clinical practice and clinical investigation of the mind and its functions, and my lifelong search for ways each of us can find our true self. This book is not only about a medicine of body, mind, and spirit; it is also about my personal odyssey from the ranks of conventional medicine to the domain of this "new" medicine, one that has been around for five thousand years, really.

My story begins at age nineteen, when a college chum gave me the book *Man Against Himself*, by Karl Menninger. After reading that book, I decided to become a psychiatrist and psychoanalyst because I wanted to learn more about the power of the mind and its effect on our lives. So I began reading Freud in college and finally realized my goals after medical school training.

Even earlier than college days, my interests had been in the mind. In childhood, together with a friend, Allen Koenigsberg, I looked into extrasensory perception and hypnosis. At that time, at thirteen, I coined a term for the experience of extrasensory phenomena: I called it "looking up." I envisioned a "great book" in the sky where all events are already recorded. At the same time,

I had an intimation of a vertical axis or vertical reality, the direction of mental ascent and descent that has been known to cultures throughout the world as the direction of movement toward freedom and away from the constraints of disease, suffering, and enslavement. Thirty-five years later, I was to learn the truth of that intuition when I discovered the world of imagination through Madame Muscat. She showed me that the vertical axis is the path to liberation and that imagination and mental imagery form the ladder by which to ascend and descend that axis.

Always looking to expand my understanding, in college I ventured into Eastern thought, with its emphasis on turning inward, and I began meditating. I also looked into the roots of my own Western religion and finally in 1974 immersed myself in the limitless realm of imagination. I then began my nine-year apprenticeship with Madame Muscat in the Western tradition of mind techniques and consciousness expansion.

All of this development led me to experience, personally and professionally, just how powerful the mind is in both the genesis and the repair of *all* illness. This understanding has been amply detailed in my previous books, *Healing Visualizations* (Bantam, 1989), *Waking Dream Therapy* (Human Sciences Press, 1981; ACMI Press, 1992), and *Studies in Non-Deterministic Psychology* (Human Sciences Press, 1980; ACMI Press, 1993). In *Waking Dream Therapy*, I present an innovative therapeutic approach to exploring our deepest selves through the power of imagination and to using sensory images that we discover during that inner journey. Through this method of using imagination, self-knowledge and self-understanding are quickly and profoundly realized, as is healing. In *Healing Visualizations*, I focus on the physical and emotional difficulties and illnesses we commonly face and offer many healing mental imagery exercises for them. *Healing Visualizations* is a primer that introduces the reader to the wondrous world of mental imagery and offers instruction on how to create your own personalized imagery.

In all my books, I use the term "mental imagery" rather than "visual imagery" or "visualization." Mental imagery implies the use of all our senses in the imagination process, not just the visual. In truth, however, visual imagery accounts for about ninety percent of all imagination events.

In this present book, I will explain which of the mind's tendencies dominate in the development of physical and emotional disturbances and which of the mind's functions prevail in the remedying of illness. In other words, I'll explain why we get ill and how we can become well. I believe that in doing so I will help the general public discover neglected avenues for genuine healing. I will introduce a new medical model, a new way of looking at illness and well-being that accepts and understands in a meaningful way the function of mind. I refer to it interchangeably as "mind medicine" or "spiritual medicine." I also hope to reintroduce the mind into psychiatry, where it has virtually disappeared from the healing process in favor of biochemical and pharmaceutical "solutions." Until now, conventional Western medicine has not been able adequately to incorporate the functions and tendencies of the mind into its model for understanding health and illness. It acknowledges a mind-body separation in our culture and believes that the mind in this equation has little or no importance in the onset or cure of disease.

This mind-body split in the Western tradition took place about 350 years ago during what was ironically called the "Age of Enlightenment," when René Descartes, the French philosopher, said that what can't be figured out by reason can't be real, and Francis Bacon, the English philosopher, said that what can't be grasped by the five senses in the external world can't be real. They and later philosophers, especially during the Industrial Revolution, relegated all nonlogical modes of thinking and nonempirical modes of perception to a purgatory of insignificance. This philosophical bomb splintered us in two—a mind-body split—and it is a trauma from which we are only now slowly recovering. In this book, I attempt to help restore and reestablish the continuity of mind and body that had been largely maintained for several thousand years before then.

Before the rupture in Western thinking took place in the seventeenth century, our forefathers perceived the world with quite a different consciousness from ours. They did not experience a separation between their consciousness and the world around them, or between each other. The worldview of the ancient, medieval, and renaissance world was of a unity. After the "Enlightenment," we began to detach ourselves from the world and each other. We split our universe in two: into the physical (all that could be directly perceived by our five senses) and the nonphysical (that which is not directly apprehensible by our senses). *Physical* became synonymous with *objective*, and *nonphysical* with *subjective. Physical* also became equated with body and reality, *subjective* with mind and unreality. These prejudices have colored our thinking until recently. Through personal experience and experimentation, I have discovered the truth of subjective reality, or more precisely, subjective realities. Imagination, mental imagery, dreams, reveries, hallucinations—these are all subjective realities. They cannot be physically measured. They can't be quantified physically. They have qualities that can't be calculated.

This book is designed to help you train your mind in a new way, to reeducate your bodymind as a whole so that you can live in a new, healthful way that is in harmony with your true nature and the world around you. It encourages you to bring healing to yourself, to participate in your own healing, by experimenting in the realm of the imagination in a way that leads to greater self-understanding.

Finally, what is new about this book and what goes beyond most of what is written and published in the mind-body field is that I am not simply presenting a set of techniques that can bring about significant change. I also provide a larger context of understanding into which these techniques fit—a social, moral, and spiritual framework that includes God, the all infinite Being from which everything we know emanates. It is said in the literature of Western wisdom that God actually made Himself smaller, drew Himself together and drew within Himself, to permit the created world to come into existence. This act of contraction was one of great mercy and love. It serves as a model by which we can understand how we may bring healing to ourselves. I shall describe this further when I discuss the healing relationship, but just knowing about this vital context of life and of how we came to be will allow the healing techniques I explain to take hold; it will help them to become imprinted indelibly in our bodyminds so that they are not just another "quick fix" but remain with us in a lasting way.

The bodymind medicine I offer here presupposes that there are nonmaterial, invisible causes and cures for all of our ills, causes that cannot be directly and objectively observed, measured, and calculated by our five senses. This is in opposition to the current Western medical model, which describes illness as being caused by "agents" of disease—specifically, microorganisms such as bacteria and viruses. No one has been able adequately to explain why some people succumb readily to these agents of disease while others do not or, if they do, why they heal more quickly. The answer lies in the invisible realm of the mind, in the imagination.

The invisible reality is synonymous with what some call the spiritual reality. It lies behind our everyday sensory reality, the visible, objective, physical reality. You discover and experience invisible reality by turning your senses inward, when you use your imagination and its functional process of mental imagery.

The invisible reality is composed of many levels or worlds, all of which are concretely real. Although they have no substantive volume or mass that we can perceive with our five senses, these worlds play a major role in informing and influencing our visible reality. These worlds are *not* simply metaphors for the outer, physical world, but are as real as this waking, physical world. This point is a major thesis of this book. I also call this invisible spiritual reality the *vertical reality*. This nonsubstantial, nonlocatable vertical reality passes its influence down into our visible reality to inform—indeed, to create—the visible, everyday world. In religio-spiritual terms, the influence of the vertical reality is seen in the creation story in the first book of Genesis. Creation came from an invisible source that prompted the appearance of our visible world. Healing is just such a creative act, requiring a movement up the vertical axis of the imagination and into the invisible spiritual reality.

People have asked me, "Do I have to believe in God or in the invisible reality in order to bring on healing?" My answer is that it is not necessary to have this belief to do the exercises and techniques I present in this book. You only need to *do* them and see what happens. As you do them, however, please suspend your skepticism and participate faithfully in the work. Many wonderful things have happened to those who have tried the mind medicine way.

The centrality given to the social and moral contexts of illness and well-being in mind or spiritual medicine is a significantly Western contribution to healing. None of the Eastern medical approaches have integrated social and mental elements into their medical practices, in spite of the Eastern acknowledgment of the extreme importance of mind in the genesis of illness. The Eastern approach is passive in effecting healing, however, whereas the Western approach is active.

In mind medicine, the mind is a full partner with the body; mind and body form a unity. When we look at our illnesses and our troubles, we assign meaning to our symptoms. We acknowledge that our symptoms have value, that they alert us not only to a bodily problem but to broader social and moral issues confronting us in our life situations. Each organ of the body has meaning on an emotional and social level when we accept the mind and body as integrated, as the ancients did.

For example, I have treated a number of patients suffering from heart disease. They came to understand and value their life experiences and see that a failure or loss of a love relationship had preceded the awareness of their heart disease. While the heart has been recognized as the seat of love since ancient days, if we view the mind and body as split, then a symptom can *never* have a meaning other than that it is a physical manifestation of a purely mechanical nature, without relevance to the emotional, mental, or social aspects of our lives. This is how conventional Western medicine views hypochondriasis, for instance, where the sufferer has multiple symptoms at one time or has persistent symptoms for which no organic disturbance can be found. Such a person is often labeled a "crock," that is, someone whose problems are "all in his mind" and therefore are not worthy of much attention. Yet the person is announcing his life suffering in the language of bodily symptoms. The body speaks in its own language about our life circumstances, expressing itself in a bodily way. All of life's experiences speak to us, whether the language be that of dreams, emotions, or bodily responses. Doctors and patients both need to learn these languages.

A patient produces symptoms until someone hears him and listens to what he is speaking about, or until he figures out his body's messages for himself. For example, suffering a shoulder problem may "speak" about shouldering problems or about carrying too much weight of responsibility on your shoulders. Similarly, a heart problem "speaks" about heartache or eating one's heart out, or being heartbroken—some problem about love reflected in the physical heart.

Essentially, then, the scientific name of an illness is not relevant in a mindbody medicine. The symptoms are important because they alert us to the fact that life factors are at work and that we have to get to the business at hand—that of searching out and correcting unhealthy tendencies. The nature of the symptom provides clues to the kind of mind processes we can use to correct the trouble. (I discuss these in Chapter 7.) In mindbody healing, however, we can study the symptoms within the intimate context of our entire life situation, because we connect the symptoms to the rest of our life. A medicine that does not incorporate the mind as meaningful will tend to isolate and separate the symptom from the person, by studying it in a detached, objective way that has no relation to the rest of our life.

*   *   *

The first chapter, "Mind Medicine," introduces you to the role of the invisible reality in health and how it functions in your life through its main invisible function, the mind. This chapter contrasts the traditional Western spiritual worldview with the current Western scientific view of reality.

Chapter 2 describes the relationship between subjective and objective reality—how they mirror each other. I apply the ancient Western idea of "as above, so below" to providing a new and workable medical model.

"The Moral Shield," Chapter 3, brings us to an awareness of the medical and healing applications of the Ten Commandments as a prescription for living a sane, sober, happy, and disease-free life.

Chapter 4 identifies and explains those mental faculties that each of us can develop to bring about our own healing. I call them the "seven keys to healing."

Chapter 5, "The Healing Relationship," gives a fresh, nourishing point of view on the significance of the relationship between healer and patient, as well as on the patient as self-healer, and how this relationship works to promote healing.

"Why We Become Ill," Chapter 6, defines the three tendencies of mind that function in each of us to create all our physical and emotional problems.

Chapter 7, "How We Become Well," provides the three remedies inherent in the functioning of our minds and hearts that act to heal our physical and emotional problems.

Chapter 8 provides a number of healing exercises using mental imagery and will.

The final chapter details my vision of what this new model of mind medicine can bring us—namely, immortality through an overcoming of disease and death, as envisioned by our ancient sages and forebears. Our movement toward this immortality or resurrective possibility comes through our inner effort and expanding consciousness rather than through dependence on medical authorities or institutions.

Throughout the book I discuss biblical stories and their relevance for our health, wellness, and realization of spirit. I must state at the outset that the Bible is a moral history of the world. It relates not so much what happened in history but the way history was lived and ways that produced the wonders and disasters that characterize life on earth. The Bible states at its beginning that an invisible, nontangible, not-apparent-to-our-five-senses reality called God created the physical world. This creation was true, perfect, beautiful, good, moral (all synonymous terms), all in the absolute sense.

To understand these biblical stories fully in their spiritual sense, I believe you must keep in mind that the stories are not to be considered *metaphors*. Metaphor, as the term has come to be understood, points to something that is real behind something that isn't real. For example, Freudian psychologists, in describing a dream event where a rifle appears, might say that the rifle really isn't a rifle, that it really is a penis. So something—a rifle—makes its appearance to our perception in a dream but is not regarded as a reality in its own right, having its own characteristics and inherent meanings. Rather, it attains significance only by what it points to—a penis—which has the "real" significance. The rifle's value merely lies in its dependence on something else, to which it relates. Its very existence depends on this relationship. The term *metaphor* denotes this dependent relationship. I would view the rifle, however, as concretely real, having value in and of itself and needing no reference point to justify its existence. It stands on its own and makes its appearance to convey some message to us via the true language of the mind—that is, through image.

The contrast between these two ways of reading image language summarizes the entire difference between a cause-and-effect dependence-based psychology like psychoanalysis and all of its derivatives, and a spiritually based self-authority-centered healing process of spiritual medicine. We need not be dependent in this life to heal. In fact, our health depends on our becoming our own authorities. Consequently, we don't use dependence-based language rooted in metaphor. Therefore, when you read about Adam and Eve challenged to decide between good and evil, you must see and feel the real people and the real choice. Bearing in mind that we accept all experience as concretely real, the Bible stories are read literally—but not *only* literally. The spiritual wisdom of Judaism holds that the Bible is to be read on four levels:

1) as concrete and literal truth
2) as analogy
3) as moral allegory
4) as an archetypal story

Abraham's migration from his home in Ur to Chaldea, for example, is recognized as a literal event. It is also, however, an analogy to an inner migration (the outer and inner reflecting each other). It is an allegory about the necessity for leaving home and the habitual environment to find our freedom; and it is an archetypal story of how we are to live our daily lives, as Abraham, who wants to find God, must do by being willing to break from the prevailing culture.

And so in this book I ask you to read the biblical references in this way. There is an invisible reality that was inhabited by Adam and Eve. Yes, they did live, as did Cain, Abel, and all the rest. When the Bible talks about people like Enoch and Elijah, who did not die, this is meant literally. These are not metaphorical stories, any more so than is Jesus' resurrection—they are all literal events. For spiritual life, *everything is at first concretely real.*

At various points along the way, I purposely reiterate certain biblical stories. I do so to remind you of their importance and to impress their meaning in your psyche. In each instance, the story serves as a means of amplifying and deepening your understanding. The repetition acts like a chant or a mantra, giving additional power to the main point of the discussion.

In connection with the biblical stories, I make reference to Eve eating the apple first and then giving it to Adam. Since in the spiritual universe nothing happens by chance, so it was not by chance that Eve tasted the fruit first. Her doing so makes a significant point in the Western spiritual tradition: *The woman is the teacher of the man.* Woman leads man into life or restores man to life. Eve leads Adam into this life on earth, which is now our university where we are to learn the laws of spiritual understanding that will one day allow us to turn this violence-ridden planet into one of love, justice, and mercy. This shift is currently taking place as the patriarchal dominance of the past gives way to the matriarchal impulse of love, wisdom, and cooperation.

A last piece of advice: Work with yourself and experiment with the techniques and methods I present to find out if they are true for you. Don't simply take my word for it. Healing is an inner journey of self-discovery that we all may undertake. Become your own authority on the subject of your health.

Mind Medicine:

Making the Invisible Visible

Before you this day there is set good and evil,
life and death. Choose life, that both you and
your descendants might live.
                    —DEUTERONOMY 30:19

Mind medicine, or spiritual medicine, is medicine
that moves us in the direction of spirit, of the invisible
reality. It is a medicine of truth and love. The original
text that inspires this book is the Bible, itself a living text
of medical healing. The essential teaching of spiritual
medicine is that we possess the means for healing ourselves through the use of our inner mental processes. We
make of ourselves our own authority and take the responsibility for our health and well-being into our own
hands. The ultimate aim of this effort is not only to attain
a state of healing but eventually to bring ourselves to a

state of longevity that presently may seem incredible. Eventually, as I hope to explicate in these pages, we might reach the point of defeating death. The possibility of resurrection is espoused by all three great Western religions, Judaism, Islam, and Christianity. This book heralds our entry into the age of resurrection spoken of in our Western spiritual tradition over many thousands of years, from ancient Egypt to Israel, Greece, Iran, Turkey, and Europe.

The twentieth century has been characterized by human death on an unprecedented scale. Mass death and the potential for even greater destruction are prompting us to try to rein in our destructive impulses. This death has been created by our own hand and can be corrected only by our own hand, but we are held in bondage when we put our trust in the authorities and leaders of this world and incorrectly believe that other human beings, or human creations, hold the key to our happiness and self-fulfillment. In misplacing our trust, we have made our universe a thoroughly dangerous place.

We can also characterize this century as the one in which we have forgotten God. Where God is, where there is truth and love, there cannot be death. God is truth and love and is stronger than death. To begin to reverse the trend of death, danger, and destruction and make of our universe a welcoming place, we have to bring God back into our lives. The coming of love and truth in this world, if we permit it, will conquer death and allow the resurrective age to reach its fulfillment.

That spirituality and religious feeling and practice play a salutary role in overcoming illness has been highlighted by Jeffrey S. Levin, associate professor of family and community medicine at Eastern Virginia Medical School, who writes as follows:

Since the nineteenth century, over 250 published empirical studies have appeared in the epidemiologic and medical literature in which one or more indicators of spirituality or religiousness, variously defined, have been statistically associated in some way with particular health outcomes. Across this literature, studies have appeared which suggest that religion is salutary for cardiovascular disease, hypertension, stroke, nearly every cancer site, colitis and enteritis, numerous health status indicators, and in terms of both morbidity and mortality. Further, this finding seems to hold regardless of how spirituality is defined and measured (beliefs, behaviors, attitudes, experiences, etc.). An especially large subliterature of over two dozen studies demonstrates the health-promotive effects of simply attending church or synagogue on a regular basis. Finally, while no one study has conclusively "proven" that a spiritual perspective or involvement in religion is a universal preventive or curative factor, significant positive health effects of spirituality have appeared in studies of whites, blacks, and Hispanics; in studies of older adults and adolescents; in studies of U.S., European, African, and Asian subjects; in prospective, retrospective, cohort, and case-control studies; in studies of Protestants, Catholics, Jews, Parsis, Buddhists, and Zulus; in studies published in the 1930s and in the 1980s; in studies measuring spirituality as belief in God, religious attendance, Bible reading, frequency of prayer, father's years of Yeshiva, numinous feelings, and history of bewitchment, among many other constructs; and in studies of self-limiting acute conditions, of fatal chronic diseases, and of illnesses with lengthy, brief, or absent latency periods between exposure and diagnosis and mortality. In short, something worthy of serious investigation seems to be consistently manifesting in these studies, and understanding the "what," "how," and "why" of this apparent spiritual factor in health . . . may be critical for reducing suffering and curing the sick.[1]

The "spiritual factor in health" that Dr. Levin mentions is *the* critical factor in all healing. This is an apt place to define the components that make up the spiritual factor and to contrast them with some of the premises underlying medicine, psychology, and science.

Chance and Divine Providence

The difference between mind medicine and conventional medicine actually lies in the perspective with which each view approaches reality. The overwhelming majority of the people in the Western world hold to the belief that chance is the fundamental reality, that the universe, although perhaps ultimately determined, is in its moment-to-moment workings an inchoate, disordered mass, random and unpredictable, and that it can perpetrate on us, at any random moment, some awful consequence. Chance is the cause of all events in a world where God does not and cannot exist.

Along with this belief comes the notion that there cannot be an invisible reality and that we are fundamentally enslaved, mechanical beings who operate in a determined manner, according to fixed cause-and-effect laws. Our job as human beings is to try to put this physical and social universe under our control, to prevent its randomness and wild unpredictability from affecting us. This belief holds that with enough knowledge at our command, we can put the universe under our dominion and that we can control, even own, the forces of nature.

Science, medicine, and psychology, three of the great institutions that rule our lives—unfortunately to excess in this era—operate in accordance with this belief in chance. In their three worldviews, it is held that human will and any nonphysical forces are subordinate to chance, which operates without the intervention of an invisible reality. Medicine says that a human being is a mere mechanism, nothing more than a mechanical organism that can be repaired whenever one of its parts breaks down. That mysterious, intangible, nonphysical element called mind is not really real and is certainly not connected with body.

Although doctors will accept that the physical can affect the mental (steroids are a case in point), fundamentally they will not accept the converse. No medicine that believes that the only reality is physical can admit or allow the nonphysical, the invisible, the mind, to be significant. Physicians in general have not the faintest idea of what role the mind plays in the genesis of disease, nor do they care. When a physician cannot find some physical pathology that "causes" a patient's complaint, he or she will usually say, "I don't find anything wrong. Your complaints are *all in your mind*. I shall send you for a psychiatric consultation."

Whatever way you slice it, from whatever angle you

view it, conventional medicine operates on the assumption that chance is the guiding principle. Even the language of medicine reveals this assumption of chance in its reliance upon statistical explanations of spontaneous remission, five-year survival rates, and genetic illness. "Spontaneous remission" means that the disappearance of an illness happened by chance, a one-in-a-million occurrence. "Five-year survival" refers to the odds that you'll be alive five years after the appearance of an illness. "Genetic illness" means that we don't understand how a disease is distributed among the members of a family except by the chance of genetic transmission. Of course, the table of chance called statistics is only an abstract reality; it doesn't say what will happen to you (unless you believe it does), and it has nothing to do with you right here at this moment.

To conventional medical science, we humans are but a chance event in the universe and just happen to have appeared here on earth. In a random world, luck explains our experience of chance—we either have "good luck" or "bad luck." Luck is a convenient explanation that takes us off the hook of responsibility for what happens to us. We see ourselves as victims of experience and take as many precautions as we can to bring security and certainty into our lives, to ensure that we don't become a "victim of circumstance." We walk around covering our heads and looking over our shoulders, worrying about the next catastrophe around the corner in this doom-and-gloom-oriented world in which the media can't wait to pounce on the next "disaster" or "tragedy" to report.

When we drop the belief in chance from our consciousness, however, we step onto the path toward spirit.

The world of invisible reality, or divine providence, looks at life in the opposite way. For those of us who believe in this worldview, the universe is ordered, operating according to a divine plan. Human beings are born with free will and have the choice to create their own reality for themselves. God's world is a paradoxical one: We are free within a determined universal or cosmic whole. *Nothing* in this world happens by chance. *Everything comes from the invisible reality and is made manifest through the actions of our will.* Even the machine world comes under the aegis of the invisible reality. If your car didn't start this morning, that didn't happen by chance. There is a reason; something had to be played out at that instant that held some significance for your life. Sometimes the significance is blatantly clear, as for people who miss a flight because of say, a mechanical failure of their car on the way to the airport, and the plane that they miss has a fatal crash.

In the perspective of spiritual reality, we read events in terms of their correspondences rather than in a cause-effect manner. Psychology, for example, would say that anxiety is causing my heart palpitations. In spiritual medicine, however, anxiety and heart palpitations correspond to each other—one is a physical manifestation, the other an emotional one, each *mirroring or reflecting* the other. They are happening simultaneously, although in our ordinary waking world of perception and experience, they seem to occur consecutively in time and thus *give the appearance* that one is causing the other.

In the scientific worldview, mind and body are split and are inherently different. (Actually, proponents of science and medicine consider the mind to be unreal.) In spiritual science and medicine, mind and body are considered to be *analogous functions* of each other. They don't cause each other; rather, they are *mirror reflections* of one another, genuine expressions of human beings. The fact that physical and emotional realities reflect each other explains why we can say, for instance, that the heart is the seat of love or the liver the seat of anger. Love reflects itself *as* heart. Heart reflects love. The heart and love are inherently connected.

So, too, is there an inherent connection between what is tangible and what is intangible. Night dreams, mental imagery, and meditation experiences are all events that are as real as our waking life events. They mirror waking-life events, as body symptoms correspond to mental and spiritual events. This is an essential point to grasp in order to understand why we become ill and how we become well.

We can understand the world in a way directly at odds with our everyday indoctrination. To be more specific: Accepting the truth of divine providence, of the mindbody unity, of the invisible reality, holds the key to attaining health.

The conventional model of reality cannot account for your or my subjective experiences, our intuitions, our spiritual desires and experiences. In dreams as well as in reveries and imaginal activity, I can find myself at the ends of the universe. My physical body is here, but I am also elsewhere at the same instant. I dreamed recently that I was at my teacher's house in Jerusalem. If you ask me: At that moment in the dream, when you were with Madame Muscat, were you closer and more vividly there and aware of being there, or were you closer to lying physically in your bed at home? If you ask such a question in reference to your own dreams, you will probably answer the question as I do: I am much more aware of and am humanly closer to my dream reality than to my bed at that time. How could it be otherwise? Who was in Jerusalem? I was. This "I" is much more than the physical body lying in the bed.

Conventional medicine and psychology cannot be

the arbiters of what is true, real, normal, and abnormal; we can't know the invisible world by means of the outer world's estimation. My dream is not open to objective scientific assessment. Science may tell me that I was in REM sleep (rapid eye movements associated with dreaming), but that tells me nothing about the truth of the dream, only about a peripheral element associated with the dream. Science cannot measure the mind, only the brain. The mind is limitless, while the brain is limited, as it is a physical object with boundaries. How can the limited house the limitless? How can the mind be in the brain, as we are led to believe it is? The limitless can give birth to the limited, can contain the limited, but it can't be the other way around. The limitless has no borders, no end.

Again, the creation story in Genesis exemplifies this theme. In the beginning there was chaos—formlessness. Out of this formlessness came the created world. In Western spiritual life, this movement from the formless and invisible to the visible is how the world actually works. This movement takes place along the axis of vertical causality. The movement of vertical causality is central to the understanding of mind medicine. Vertical causality defines the relationship of the invisible world to the visible world. In the invisible reality there are levels of creation, as illustrated by the diagram on page 10.

In consciousness, these levels of creation are all mirroring each other simultaneously. That's how we experience vertical reality. Take, for example, a possibility called walking. The knowledge for fulfilling this possibility comes as an *impulse* that is registered as an *idea*, which is seen as an *image*, and is experienced as an *action*. Each of these functions mirrors the others. In our everyday life, we are usually aware of the reality of the action but not of the other three.

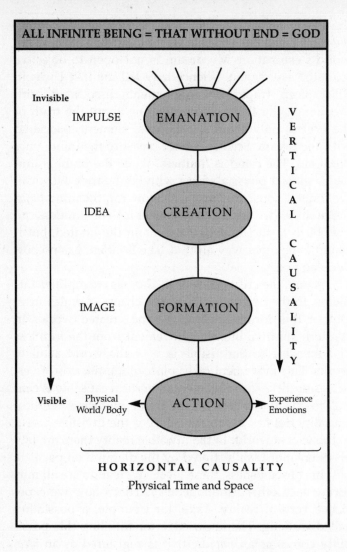

The causality that underlies the understanding of natural science and our conventional medicine is "horizontal causality," whose central focus is visibility. According to conventional medicine, physical causes have physical effects. For instance, a microorganism causes disease, while changes in the biochemistry of the brain cause mental illness. Thus, physical causes can give rise to both physical and nonphysical responses.

From the vertical causality perspective, diseases arise from the formless realm of mind mediated by images, ideas, and beliefs, which then materialize in the physical world. For instance, an infection at the physical level mirrors the breakdown of the moral and social fabric of our existence. Healing then must involve the other levels of vertical causality: Our own healing of our physical symptoms will involve the healing of the context in which we live our lives.

Vertical causality lies at the foundation of Judaism and Christianity. In the spiritual life of the West, the intersection of the vertical and horizontal is represented by the following sign: +. The cross of Christianity speaks to the vertical and horizontal interplay. For Christian spirituality, Jesus is at the intersection of the vertical and horizontal: ✝.Jesus

Also for Western spirituality, the interplay and interrelation of above and below is designated by the Star of David: ✡. "As above, so below" is the spiritual shorthand for the law of analogy, for the inherent relationship of two things that don't seem to be connected at first glance. Thus, "as above, so below" alludes to the influence of the vertical worlds on the human world and vice versa. For spiritual understanding, matter and spirit are analogies of each other. The upward triangle in the Star of David ($\triangle$) not only represents above but also is the symbol for fire. The downward triangle (∇), not only represents below but also is the symbol for water. Additionally, the symbol △ symbolizes air, while the symbol ▽ symbolizes earth. The four elements represent the constituent elements in their melding and blending with each other, out of which all living matter in our universe is composed.

The vertical reality is a timeless realm, the experience of the eternal moment or instant. It is what physicists call "no time," in which we may be witness to the presence of the present. This eternal moment is then played out along the horizontal axis of past, present, and future as the narrative of our lives and as what we perceive as cause-and-effect experience, ending eventually in death. The focus in mind medicine is to establish our connection with the presence of the present and come back to the vertical reality as the sustainer of our life, the place where true healing happens. The techniques of mind medicine allow us the possibility of living in "no time" and thereby aligning and attuning ourselves with the vertical reality. This vertical reality is the realm of freedom, the realm of love, the realm of morality, the realm of God. What happens there has its impact in time and is lived out in the world of time. Miracles can be defined in exactly this way, as happenings without precedent or antecedent (that is, out of time) and having effects in the world of historical time. The Red Sea parting and Jesus being resurrected are two miraculous instances that have had effects lasting thousands of years.

In the following chart I have summarized the twelve paths of providence and the twelve paths of chance. Each is part of a road that we can choose to follow, leading either to life or to death respectively.

12 Paths to Life *Providence* Vertical Causality	12 Paths to Death *Chance* Horizontal Causality
Mindbody unity	Mind-body split
Grace	Luck
Being (present)	Expectation (future)
Creator	Victim
Belief creates experience	Experience creates belief
Objective and subjective reality both exist	Only objective reality exists
Analogic-intuitive thought supplemented by logic	Logic the only valuable thought process, equated with truth
Reality and truth not the same	Reality and truth the same
Maintain self-authority	Surrender authority to someone else
Faith	Skepticism
Form follows function	Function follows form
Resurrection	Death

The road of providence is linked directly to processes that acknowledge the primacy of vertical causality, while the road of chance is linked directly to processes that acknowledge the primacy of horizontal causality.

Most of the paths listed in the chart will be discussed in this chapter, the rest in the following chapters. Let's look now at some comparisons between vertical and horizontal thinking.

Logic and Truth

In the world of chance—that is, horizontal causality—the glue that is used to tie things together is logic, an intellective function that deals only with the seen, the tangible, the quantitative. It excludes any phenomenon that cannot be experienced directly in the physical world or that operates outside scientific laws—like miracles.

This dependence on logic is misleading and false. Something can be true and yet not have a basis in formal logic, while something based on formal logic can be quite false. For this reason, spiritual medicine deals not with logic but with truth. In 1989, I appeared on the Geraldo Rivera TV show with two other healers. We each brought on five patients who had undergone healing for serious physical illnesses, including cancer. In the audience were dozens of other people who had also undergone healing. A conventional physician appeared on the show to explain to the audience that what they were witnessing was not true because it didn't conform to the laws of logic. The way she stated it was that all the healing that was directly experienced was "only anecdotal," meaning that it was not valid, genuine, or real, since it was "only" subjective and had not been confirmed by "true" objective, scientific scrutiny via a double-blind controlled study. What she was saying made some sense in the abstract—for instance, with regard to testing medicines in a laboratory. But it certainly did not speak to the truth of those who had been healed. For the physician, proof had to be based not on what the patients' senses directly confirmed for them but on a preconceived idea of what makes something true. She was so taken by her preconceived idea that she could not accept the truth staring her in the face. It is characteristic of human nature in general that many preconceived ideas are formed early in life and are cultivated on the ground of logical deduction. Subsequently, whatever we encounter that doesn't fit our logical framework is discarded as worthless. The truth of the healings that all those people experienced defies current logical or medical explanation and so cannot be accepted. Thus, truth loses out to preconceived skepticism.

For instance, I know about the case of a youngish man who developed carcinoma of the head of the pancreas. He underwent surgery, and the head of the pancreas was removed. His doctors noted some spread of the cancer to superficial layers of the adjacent portal vein and one adjacent lymph node, but everything else in the area was clean and normal, including ten lymph nodes farther up in the chain and farther away from the head of the pancreas. His cancer marker blood test was also normal. He was then offered a combination of chemotherapy and radiation as a "preventive" medical program. The course of this program was described to him as going through a "second surgery." The doctors considered it necessary because there *could* be one cancer cell floating around his system that was not detectable by any known means. The rationale for this devastating intervention, which ended up destroying one kidney, was that there was a "chance" a cancer cell was hanging out somewhere. Here is nineteenth-century germ theory applied to a chronic disease situation: An isolated cell, like a bacterium, can land and grow somewhere and "cause" illness. This doubt on the doctor's part that the cancer was gone was conveyed to the patient, who was then filled with terror that the cancer would return. The patient then lived out of that implanted belief. He lived out his days feeling powerless to make any potentially beneficial changes, such as social or moral changes, changes in diet, prayer, and so on.

Another distinction between logic and truth involves the difference between what is and what may be. Logic bases its propositions on what is called "if-then" thinking. *If* so-and-so is the cause, *then* such-and-such is the likely outcome. Truth, however, always concerns itself with what is, with what presents itself to us and our perceptions in the immediacy of the present moment. Logical thinking projects into the future: making predictions, drawing conclusions, gauging outcomes. The trouble is that *the future doesn't exist*—it is simply potential. It hasn't happened yet. To treat it otherwise is to participate in an illusion. Every notion we have that the future can be predicted, manipulated, shaped, or otherwise controlled is untrue. We waste the bulk of our lives buying into this illusory realm that can never belong to us. Struggling with what is fundamentally false takes a heavy toll on our physical and emotional lives. We play a continuous game, like the story of the emperor's new clothes, giving a special role to the institutions of science, medicine, and psychology and to their keepers, who themselves believe their own mirages and are enjoying the power this falsehood gives them.

In mind medicine, the future belongs *only* to God. The First Commandment says: "You shall have no other gods before me." The Sufis (Islamic mystics) say the same thing rather beautifully: "Don't put any other god before God." Scientists and physicians who presume to

predict the future or who are concerned with the outcomes of their experiments want to put themselves in
the place of God, usurp His knowledge and power, and
create idol worship. If you want to heal, get out of the
future and get back to the present.

*The essence of spiritual medicine is encapsulated in one
act, and all healing is based in one act: Come into the present.*
Leave the personal past. What happened, happened already. It is dead, gone, buried. It is in the realm of finished experience. Hanging on to it is to perpetuate your
enslavement. If-then thinking trades on the idea that
your past experience dictates your future experience: If
this was the pattern in the past, then this is the way the
future has to be. This way of thinking leaves you no
options and perpetuates your enslavement. We cling to
this way of thinking to help us fix the future, to gain
control of it, because we believe that the future is real
and that we can know it. Abandon the future, abandon
the past. Put your trust in the moment, in the instant, in
the presence of the present, and watch your life become
freer than you have ever known it.

Some of you who are new to spiritual thinking may
be murmuring that I am "deep-sixing" logical thought,
but that is not at all the case. Rather, I am assigning an
appropriate place to deductive logic, as a support for
intuition, to that inductive, inner ana-logic that speaks
to us as our first voice, *always* in the present tense and
that comes from our heart or our gut—as in "gut feeling." Once our intuition has informed us, then we can
use our logic to implement the action that our intuition
impels us toward. At present in this man-made world,
our logical processes have run wild in a technological
ecstasy that is devastating our environment. Unre-
strained logic that believes it can triumph over God and
that leads us to believe we are God is analogous to can-

cer. Cancer is the body running wild. Logic is the intellect running wild. We cannot bring cancer under control unless we can bring our intellect under control; nor can we remedy environmental disaster spawned by technology in the name of progress and the "American dream" unless we acknowledge the truth of our own dreams, our inner and greater spiritual realities.

Truth and Reality in Healing

In mind medicine we accept the existence of all experience as real, both in the inner forum of consciousness—in dreams, fantasies, hallucinations, imagination, thoughts, feelings, and sensations—and in the outer forum of consciousness known as the external world, including the world of nature and the man-made. Anxiety is real, anger is real, dreams are real, hallucinations are real, fear is real. For us *everything* is real, but mind medicine looks beyond what is real to what is true. The focus in conventional medicine, however, is on the real but not on the true. This is one of the most crucial differences between our mind medicine and conventional medicine—namely, the former says that *reality and truth are not the same*.

Reality means the existence of any phenomena that we perceive or create in either the outer or inner world. Truth means what is, what is fact, and *what is valid within a given context*. For instance, anxiety is real and is even true for you at the moment that you feel it. But *its context is not true*. All anxiety is about the future. If you feel anxious, ask yourself, "What am I anxious about?" Similarly, if you feel fearful, nervous, tense, worried, or angry, ask yourself the corresponding question. Or do the same for someone you are with who is experiencing these distressing feelings. The answer that comes back will *always* be about something that is related to the future. But the future does not exist! It is only potential and has not happened. It is by its nature false, and any discussion of or emotion connected with the future is not true. So though the anxiety is real, its context is untrue. The same may be said about disquieting feelings related to the past, such as guilt, shame, regret, and vengeance. They are all real and true at the moment, but what they refer to, the context in which they are operating, is not true. The past is illusory, gone, finished, dead, out of existence. Like the future, it is not true. It was and is not now. Holding on to the past simply generates thoughts about the future: "Since it was like that in the past, it has to be like that again in the future." That is how we are trained to think, and this thinking is the basis for the notion that experience (past) creates belief (future). (This false notion will be discussed in detail in the next chapter.)

A psychiatrist, psychologist, or other clinician who judges that some form of expression in another person is unreal denies the reality of that other person's experience, making the person feel misunderstood and unwelcome, at some level of being, in his or her relationship with the clinician. That misunderstanding is unresolvable because the clinician has a preconceived idea of what is real. In fact, all psychiatric diagnostic labels are based on the clinician's assessment of the patient's relationship to "reality." For example, the experience of a schizophrenic who claims that he is Jesus Christ is quite real, but it isn't true. Hence the psychiatric term *delusion*, meaning "unreal," is misleading. The schizophrenic's experience is real but not true. By missing this point psychiatry has severely curtailed its effectiveness, so much so that the profession has essentially been reduced to pill-pushing, making it just another subdivision of biochemistry.

Psychiatrists generally regard people who don't conform to their preconceived standards of normal and abnormal as emotionally disturbed. Thus, they essentially regard hallucinations as not real or "crazy," when in truth they are quite real and the hallucinator is certainly experiencing them as such. To tell him or her otherwise further demeans and devalues the person and contributes toward driving him or her deeper into his illness. Unfortunately, psychiatry has not been able substantially to get past this barrier and so cannot even begin to grapple with the distinction between truth and reality. Understanding this distinction can be the initial step toward reclaiming the arena of mind for psychiatry, which is the promise that psychiatry held out for itself and those sufferers called patients before it relinquished its legitimacy as a field of inquiry and therapy in order to accommodate itself to and be accepted by our materially based conventional medicine.

In mind medicine, we never question the *reality* of a person's experience. What we question is its *truth*. A person approached in this way will soon begin to want to make changes and will set about doing so through one or more techniques that put the person on the road to healing. It seems that we humans have a built-in desire to be in truth, and we will work to serve that truth. But if you try to tell me what's real, I may put up a great fight or, conversely, become compliant and bow down before your authority. Neither possibility would bode well for my welfare. Yes, we may also fight about what's true, but we can experiment and reach some accord through experimentation. This is what mind medicine is about: We don't submit to any outside authority, and we experiment with what we discover to find out if it is true. When we practice in this way, we achieve remarkable results in short order. People become able to progress constructively with their lives.

In the physical realm mind medicine is also concerned with reality and truth. I don't for one minute think that physical expressions of illness should be denied or neglected. If I did, I would be making the same error as the physicians who deny the reality of physical symptoms when no "organic cause" can be discovered. We have to engage the symptoms by embracing them, even thanking them for making their appearance so as to alert us and give us an opportunity to make significant changes in our lives. They are part of a whole picture of mindbody integration within the context of our social and moral relationship to the world.

The Will to Power and the Will to Love

Truth and logic are mirrored by love and power, respectively. Truth and love are provided to us and through us by the invisible reality, while logic and power, which aim at controlling the future, have evolved from the human mind by dint of our choices. The interplay of logic and power is illustrated by Adolf Hitler's heinous book *Mein Kampf*, which sought to show logically that the Jews were responsible for all the troubles of the Germans and that the way out of those troubles was to exterminate the Jews. His "logic," of course, was based on a false belief. False belief is at its basis a will to power, an unnatural megalomania that attempts to supplant even God.

The origin of the false belief that engenders the will to power goes back to the archetypal story of Adam and Eve in the Garden of Eden. In this paradise there is no disease and no death, only eternal life and happiness as promised our first parents by God, who tells them that Eden is theirs for eternity, if only they listen to His voice and do not eat the fruit of the Tree of Knowledge of Good and Evil. In this paradise, the couple is visited by the serpent, who makes Eve a proposition that is very difficult to refuse. *He promises her that she and Adam will be able to usurp the knowledge and power of God and thereby gain omniscience of the future and omnipotence over the future and, consequently, like God, become immortal.* All they have to do is eat the fruit of the Tree of Knowledge. Eve is thrown into a terrible quandary by this offer. She is torn between listening to God's voice or to the serpent's voice, which promises a future reward based upon giving in to the experience of the fruit. Eve finally resolves the conflict by going for the fruit. The rest is the history of the world.

Today, the serpent represents all of the individuals, authorities, and institutions that live by the will to power and the inherent promise in that will that we shall control our future, otherwise known as destiny. But all the while those same individuals, institutions, and authorities are trying to control our destiny for us. The serpent lied to Eve and Adam, and we all labor under the same lie proffered to us by the agents of the serpent, who promise us what inherently can never be our mandate—namely, to usurp the knowledge and power of God.

Truth and love are analogous in the Western spiritual tradition. There has always been a conflict in the West between the will to power and the will to love. The will to power comes from the impulse to usurp the knowledge and power of God. Our belief that we are God is megalomania. The urge toward superhuman status represents the tragic side of the Western tradition that sees the world as meaningful and as the context for actions that can either benefit or destroy us.

When in our grandiosity or megalomania we stumble over the First and Second Commandments—First, You shall not have any Gods before me; Second, You shall not make a graven image and not bow down before any graven image or created idol—we lose our way. Above all, our *humility* atrophies. The subverting of humility brings disaster into our individual human existence and can even spell disaster for a larger social community as well, as in the case of Hitler, Jim Jones, Idi Amin, and Saddam Hussein, to name but a few. Such destruction serves the will to power, which requires that the one seeking power subjugate or dominate others in some discernible way.

The physician I met on the Geraldo Rivera show seemed to exhibit an absence of loving-kindness toward those who had been healed. She negated their experiences. They had all come out of love for what they had received from God, but the physician met them with an attitude that said: "Don't believe what has happened to you and what your senses are directly telling you." In truth, she told them that they were crazy for believing something and experiencing something that did not conform to a man-made scientific standard. She devalued and demeaned their experience in an apparently unloving manner.

Love is the nutrient force of the invisible reality that makes truth and morality possible, and at the head of that reality stands God. Love, showering from above to below, permits the created world of the earth to continue functioning. Each of us is infused with the capacity to perpetuate this life energy by acting as its agent here on earth. Nothing that comes into contact with this monumental force can die. Consequently, contrary to popular belief, we are not meant to die as a "natural" ending to the process of birth and development. We are meant to live—in fact, to live forever. Death is a process we impose on our own freedom, for we are the only beings capable of integrating with our inborn capacity to live forever—to overcome death, as it were.

God never meant for anyone to die. He has wept ceaselessly for us since the fall from Eden, and in His everlasting and unswerving love He has steadfastly remained devoted to us and to our efforts to reach Him. When our efforts fail, we are then swept away by the great surgeon called death, so that we may begin the cycle all over again.

Acting out of love, in accord with the moral standards presented to us from the beginning and rooted in serving truth, gives us the way to overcome death. It is only out of love that we are moral toward each other. The commandments are teaching tools that define our relationship to each other and to God. Every act of moral correctness comes out of the will to love. Conversely, every deviation from moral correctness comes out of the will to power. It is love that makes us behave in the likeness of God.

There will be much more to say about love elsewhere in this book, but it has to be noted here that love is a necessary ingredient in spiritual medicine. It is the nutritive force of the universe and the emanation from the heart of God. I have seen untold suffering and unhappiness manifested in the absence of love. We need to be loving. We may need to be loved as well, but lovingness is the key ingredient. The absence of loving in our lives sets the stage for incredible grieving, "quiet desperation," abject sadness, and depression that can manifest as serious physical illness as well. It is well known that love is strong as death, that love can even conquer death. The will to love serves the force of life, while the will to power serves the force of death.

How does this clear dichotomy come about? The answer starts with God, as it always does in a spiritually based medicine. God came and said that at every moment in life, we would be faced with choosing life or choosing death. We choose our own path—life or death. Choosing the path of death means clinging to anything that is *not* connected with the present moment. This includes holding on to the past, believing that the future is real, accepting man-made standards as true, genuine, and worth striving for, letting logic take the place of truth, believing that outside authorities hold the answers to our existence, putting some god before God, and a myriad of other mistakes that are discussed at other points in this book. Choosing any direction that denies the reality of the invisible spiritual dimension and the reality of the present moment as the only truth consigns us to the domain of death. For now, as we move on to the next chapter, we will take a closer look at the domain of life, at vertical causality and its influence in our lives.

2

The Mirrored Universe

There is nothing either good or bad, but thinking
makes it so.
                    —SHAKESPEARE, *Hamlet*, II.2

The vertical, spiritual reality operates through our
individual consciousness by manifesting inner perceptions as outer, physical experiences. The inner creates the
outer. Belief creates experience. The invisible gives birth
to the visible. Each of us reflects in our personal life experience what is true on a cosmic, universal level: "As
above, so below."

Mirroring

Within the vertical reality is everything insubstan-
tial as well as everything substantial. Fine, nonsubstan-

tial matter, termed "absolute matter" by the Sufi mystics, moves down the vertical ladder to more and more substantial matter until it becomes the fully substantial gross matter characteristic of our physical world. This movement, as depicted in the diagram on page 10, is from emanation to creation to formation to action (the physical world).

Coincident with the birthing of physical matter from invisible, absolute matter is a process of reflecting. That is, each level reflects the other levels. Thus, the visible physical world is a reflection of the invisible, nonmaterial world. Reflecting is the same process as mirroring—indeed, to mirror is to reflect. To be made in the image of God is to be a reflection, a mirror of God. It is not to be the same as God. When we look into a mirror, we are seeing a reflection, a likeness, not a sameness. We are like God, but we are not the same as God.

Mirroring is of fundamental importance in spiritual medicine. One important aspect of mirroring has to do with analogy. Analogy refers to the relationship between two things that have points of likeness but that are not the same. Analogy is a function of thinking in wholes, seeing the whole of something. For instance, when I put my left hand up to the mirror, my right hand is reflected back. What I am observing is analogy. These two hands are alike, but they are not the same. At the same time, they represent the *totality* of handedness. We can see the front, back, left, right of the hands *at the same instant.*

Thus, analogical thinking grasps wholeness in the instant, while logical thinking tends to dissect an experience, breaking it down into parts, hoping by the inferences drawn from such a process to put together the whole picture *over time.*

In analogical thought, the two related elements do

not even have to be of the same nature—for instance, they don't have to be two physical things. The heart and love may be viewed as analogous: One is physical, while the other is a passion, not a physical object. We can say that the heart is the physical analogue of love. The heart mirrors (reflects) love in the physical world and the physical body (witness the depiction of hearts on valentines). Mental images and physical things can also be analogues of each other. For instance, you may mentally image a chair or you may see a chair in the physical world. These two chairs are both three-dimensional, but the mental image has no volume or mass, while the physical chair does. Hence, they are analogies of each other.

We are beginning to see here a way of thinking other than logic, a way called analogical thinking. In analogical thinking, one thing doesn't *cause* the next. Rather, one thing *correlates* or *corresponds to* the next, as in the heart and love example. Love didn't cause the heart; each exists in its own domain, but each reflects the other.

Analogical thinking allows us to find meaning in our life situations that is quite different from that which we discern by analyzing. The latter is based on cause-and-effect thinking aimed at reaching a fixed conclusion, whereas analogizing leads to a revelatory response.

The realm of science offers an analogy to the mirroring function and the movement from invisibility to visibility. In 1948, Dennis Gabor, a Hungarian physicist working in the field of optics, developed a process of lensless photography that he called "holography," for which he won the Nobel Prize in 1953. In an experiment designed to demonstrate the process, Gabor shined a laser beam through a semimirror, half dark, half silver. This split the beam in two parts, which were deflected in two directions. One beam, called the reference beam, was sent directly to a photographic plate as a pattern of energy. The other beam, called the working beam, was deflected off additional semimirrors, then deflected off an object (as happens in ordinary photography), and finally was directed to the same photographic plate, where it met the reference beam and was registered also as a pattern of energy, not as an image. On the photographic plate, *the visible image (that is, the working beam, which carried the reflection of the object) melded with an invisible ground or matrix* looking thus:

Gabor then fired a laser beam at the photographic plate. Amazingly, behind the plate appeared a three-dimensional image of the object suspended in space. He then broke the plate on the floor into fragments and shined a laser at one fragment. Again, the three-dimensional image appeared suspended in space. If the plate had been broken further into fragments and a laser fired at any one fragment, the three-dimensional image would still have appeared, but less distinctly. Thus, as this analogy shows, any part *contains* the whole. In fact, some physicists believe that this holographic analogy applies to the universe as a whole.

Inner and outer experiences—from mental images and dreams to ordinary sense perceptions—are both analogous to the invisible reality. By attending to these reflections of the invisible that unfold before and within us, we gain knowledge of that invisible reality. That knowledge expands and enlarges our consciousness and can help us heal ourselves of illnesses and other life problems.

Knowing that the part contains the whole has a good deal of practical application. We can use it in our mind medicine to provide a gnosis rather than a diagnosis.[1] To *diagnose* means "to analyze, to split apart," and then to form a whole picture by inferring what the elements mean. *Gnosis* leads to a higher form of knowledge; it means investigation into vital concerns by methods having a spiritual component. Often, gnosis involves an intuitive process that lets us see the whole picture, including correspondences and reflections, in a single instant. Returning to our analogy, we can say that intuition provides us with a holographic picture, as do gnostic healing techniques such as foot reflexology, iridology (the study of the iris), and auricular therapy (the study of the ear). All these techniques give a map reading of the entire body by looking at a single organ.

Morphology, the science and study of the face, the outer image, is a five-thousand-year-old medical tradition that is also holographic in nature. Just as the mental imagery that we experience is a reflection of the spiritual reality, the face is the external reflection of our inner beliefs. In fact, every inner and outer image is a hologramlike event revealing correspondences between inside and outside.

From the spiritual medicine point of view, anxiety and ulcer correspond to each other, as do anger and hypertension. Understanding them in gnostic, holistic terms requires that our interventions take into account our entire life, *all* levels of our lived existence: physical, emotional, mental, social, moral, and spiritual. If we are anxious, it means that our body is out of balance. When we recognize our anxiety, we must also consider its source in social, moral, and spiritual factors. For example, a social factor might be the need to compete, a moral factor the need to control the future by setting up expectations, and a spiritual factor the tendency to live away from the present moment and not trust in the beneficence of the invisible reality. Thus, gnostic investigation of just one symptom (anxiety) can reveal an entire picture of our life.

Every holographic-type event is a glyph, a language of form and wholeness, like the Egyptian hieroglyphs, revealing a wealth of hidden information. And every experience, whether it takes place in the outer world of everyday reality, in the inner world of subjective consciousness, or in the dream reality during sleep, is holographic, reflecting its truths in the glyphic images that parade before our senses. When we learn to think analogically and train ourselves to read the holographic images, we begin to experience a sense of lightness and freedom. We feel our burdens become lighter, and we feel less dependent on outside authority.

In order to train ourselves to read and understand our bodies' symptoms and our life experiences, we must learn to see that everything has a correlation or correspondence. Then we need to translate this perception into information that is looked at analogically rather than logically. Thinking analogically doesn't draw us into making conclusions immediately. When we don't jump to conclusions, we are not running into the future. When we stop our thoughts from moving into the future, we stop the emotional responses of anxiety, worry, and fear. These emotions are *always* concerned with the future. When we still these emotions, we also stop the corresponding physical responses that produce wear and tear on the body.

A man with cancer came to see me because of his

anxiety about how he was going to live out the rest of his life. His doctors had told him that he had little time to live. He was a creative man who wanted to continue his work, but now felt, "What's the use?" He experienced himself as being deprived of the value of his creativity after having been told that his death was imminent. For him, this was a useless piece of information—actually a piece of disinformation, since no human being knows how long he or she is going to live. He wanted some peace of mind.

We embarked on an imagery exercise called "Finding the Room of Silence." I asked him to imagine himself in a room together with his anxiety and fear. He was then to turn his back on the fear and anxiety, find the door out of that room, and go into another room with the intention of eventually finding a room of silence. He did so. I asked him to explore that room of silence. He found a picture on the wall of a shepherd with lambs. I asked him to go into that picture and become the shepherd. He led the lambs into a meadow, where he saw a valley into which he descended. He felt much calmer and more peaceful in the valley, and he found a person who was very kind to him and who was ready to listen calmly to his anxiety about life. He felt quite comfortable in this person's presence. He returned feeling much better than before he had started.

I asked him if there was anyone around him who he felt was not giving him the proper emotional support. He said that one person to whom he felt especially close was "trying to *get* me to feel better." He understood that this person's attitude would not benefit him because if he failed to feel better, he would be letting that person down and thereby would increase his own suffering. He was at a loss as to what to do, and his face bore a look of dejection at that point. As he was dependent on that person as well, he was quite concerned about losing that person's care and interest.

In imagery work, I differentiate inner life from waking life. Most of us call waking life "real life," but this implies that our other experiences are unreal, including not only imaginal life but dream life, fantasy life, hallucinatory life, reverie life—in short, *all* inner experiences. But I believe that imagery experience corresponds to everyday experience. My patient's inner image was speaking to an analogous situation in his life where he was not being treated with understanding. I paid attention to the correspondence that exists between inner and outer life. I read the images, and something in me was stirred so that I experienced an intuition. When I conveyed my impression to the patient, he confirmed that what was happening in the imaginal experience was not happening in his waking life. He was missing that kind of caring; and his inner experience gave him the clue to what was creating the anxiety.

Here is another example of an inner image that can be seen as a hologram or glyph, to be read for clues about healing. Meg* was a young woman who suffered from some nagging physical difficulties, including painful breast cysts and an overactive thyroid. She was intelligent and humorous, though somewhat high-strung. She complained of a lifelong fear of snakes and had had recurrent dreams about them throughout her life, particularly in her childhood.

I pointed out to her that when she looked into the mirror of her interior life, she would see reflected back

---

*Names and identifying details of people who have worked with me mentioned throughout the book have been changed to protect the individual's privacy.

to her a quality or characteristic embodied as a snake. "What are snakes?" I asked her. (Snakes are rich in meaning; they can represent knowledge, healing, evil, instinctual sexual forces, spiritual awakening, temptation, and seduction.) She responded that the snakes of her dreams had to do with evil. They were for her evil impulses from which she was fleeing—the "snake in the grass," so to speak.

I thought it would be worthwhile for her to contemplate those impulses in herself that she might be denying and that were being mirrored to her by snakes. She at first recoiled from this notion but then recognized that she had had many experiences recently with a number of people who turned out to be "snakes in the grass." She was well aware that nothing happens by chance, and in everyday life she recognized the mirroring, but she had failed to apply that to her dream life.

Given all the connections between snakes and "evil" impulses, I asked her to pay attention to these impulses in herself over the next week and accept their presence. When she returned a week later, she was quite amazed at what she had discovered was going on in her mind. She had become aware that she herself had been thinking about stealing, cheating, and lying. She now could accept that she had these impulses without judging herself adversely. With this new-found self-acceptance, she had had one of the quietest weeks she had ever known. By owning these previously rejected qualities, she could now disown them. With acceptance comes control over thoughts and impulses: We cannot disown what we don't own. Since that time, she has had only one other disturbing snake dream that we read right away and cleared up. Her breast cysts have disappeared, and her thyroid function has been normal.

Belief Creates Experience

The vertical, spiritual reality explains another critical concept in mind medicine. Beliefs are ideas that arise in the level of creation in the vertical reality. As beliefs filter down to the level of formation, they are reflected as images. Images in turn filter down to the level of the physical world, the world of action, where they are reflected as experiences. This picture can be conceptualized in a way that reverses our ordinary way of looking at our relation to the world—namely, the vertical reality model leads to the concept that *beliefs create experience.*[2] Other ways of putting the same idea are that the invisible gives rise to the visible, the inner creates the outer, and thoughts create action by means of images. Its corollary is that experiences reflect the beliefs that engendered them. Thus, the usual idea that our beliefs arise out of our experiences is exactly the opposite of the truth embodied in the vertical reality. Experiences can confirm our beliefs, but not birth them. The reason our culture inculcates in us the idea that experience creates belief is that it views beliefs as subjective, not measurable or directly observable, whereas experiences are manifested in our physical body via our five senses.

The origin of the idea that belief creates experience is found in the biblical story of Adam naming the animals in the Garden. When Adam named the animals, he understood that *form follows function.* When he wanted to name and concretize courage, he called it "lion." When he wanted to name and concretize gentleness, he called it "lamb." When he wanted to name and concretize peacefulness, he called it "dove."

Adam's way of naming goes directly counter to the very widely held but false belief that form gives rise to function, that the visible and material substance gives rise to the nonmaterial aspects of human experience. For example, a scientist laboring under this false belief would say that we see because we have eyes and that we smell because we have a nose. This way of thinking underlies practically all scientific, medical, and psychological thinking in modern times in the West. The idea that we see because we have eyes is an example of cause-and-effect thinking, a way of saying that experience (something physical, tangible) creates belief (something nonmaterial).

In contrast, Adam demonstrates the mirroring process by naming according to the idea that form follows function. In terms of mind medicine, we would say that having eyes fulfills the function of seeing, having a nose fulfills the function of smelling, and having wings fulfills the function of flying. The invisible quality or function gives rise to the physical characteristic. The basic premise that belief creates experience informs all spiritual practice everywhere.

The analogy with holography is also relevant to the realm of belief. For example, suppose that a boy has a belief that he needs a girl, while a girl has the belief that she is ready to meet a boy. These beliefs give rise to the experience the two people have of meeting in some set of circumstances. In this case, the experience materializes from the boy's active will meeting the girl's passive, receptive will and presents itself to them as a sensory reality.

Here is another example. A man has the belief that he must steal. Another man has the belief that he can be stolen from, that life is dangerous. These two beliefs meet and the result is the experience of a robbery. In mind medicine, every experience represents the meeting of two beliefs.

The simple idea that belief creates experience is

what the so-called "New Age" consciousness is groping toward in our Western culture. The New Age is reaching out to touch the "Old Age"—the living tradition of the ancient spiritual doctrines, just as Adam reaches for the animating hand of God on the ceiling of the Sistine Chapel. This simple idea is so profound, so liberating, that established authorities everywhere seek to suppress it, because it opens the door to the personal freedom that we have been seeking ever since Eve bit the apple. The idea is clearly stated at the beginning of Genesis, where the creation of the world is described as a movement of God's will: "And God said, Let there be light: and there was light." The movement of will is tantamount to a belief giving rise to a creation. What is created is synonymous with experience.

When Adam and Eve left Eden, they descended to the physical level of reality called earth. Eden had been a nonphysical reality where there was no death and no disease. There was unending belief—the kind that translates into the certainty of faith in God. It was the place where God's will was joined to our primordial progenitors. It was there that belief was formed. When human life came to this earth, it carried the means whereby it could resurrect itself to that paradisiacal existence. The means is the knowledge that belief creates experience, although this is a forgotten fact within the life context of most people. In order to gain relief from pain and suffering, we must remember—must *know*—that belief creates experience. This is the first big step to personal salvation. For we are all Adam and Eve, have all come here because we have bitten the apple and are holding to the primacy of experience over belief, which keeps us enslaved to the material-physical world.

In the Garden of Eden, Eve is tempted by the serpent, who promises her the unlimited power and knowledge of God if she will eat the apple from the Tree of Knowledge of Good and Evil. As we have seen, she then enters into a state of great doubt, having given ear to a second voice that makes her question her faith in the one voice of God.

Eve accepts the serpent's offer, intending to usurp the role of God and arrogate to herself and Adam the omnipotence and omniscience of God—to have control over events, to have knowledge of the future, and to be immortal. Having given in to the doubt engendered by the serpent's offer, Adam and Eve then find themselves in constant doubt, because their attempt to usurp God's role has enormous consequences. They are driven from the Garden into the physical realm of death, disease, and unhappiness, and the fear that this event generates makes them—and all of us—desperate to change those circumstances.

Each of us has accepted the serpent's offer, which appeals to our yearning to have the unlimited power of God. We adhere to two fundamental beliefs engendered by the serpent, and these beliefs are the principal obstacles to the achievement of freedom and self-realization. One of these beliefs we have already described: Experience creates belief. The other is that the purpose of living is to arrive at a nondisturbed state by gaining pleasure and avoiding pain. Now, stop for a moment and reflect on this. At first glance, don't you agree with those two beliefs? Isn't it also exquisitely paradoxical that the belief that experience creates belief is actually a belief about experience and as such is a belief that creates experience?

These two beliefs tie us to pain and suffering and make it possible for us to be enslaved by other people. These beliefs hypnotize us into thinking that the physical plane of existence—the world of experience created ceaselessly by each of us—contains the things that will make us happy, the things upon which we must depend in order to be happy. We habitually identify with the things, objects, designations of this world, creating the illusory idea that these objects and the "I" that identifies with them are identical. That is, we habitually identify the creator with his or her creation. We believe we are what we have and what we have created. And because worldly events, experiences, and circumstances appear to be coming from outside and imposing themselves on us, we believe they are happening to us and fail to notice that we ourselves are creating them.

Of course, neither of these two fundamental beliefs about reality is true. They do not describe the way reality works. The discovery that they are not true can be shattering for some, while it can fill others with the most serene peace; in some, it can provoke a profound belly laugh, while still others may have all of these responses at once. Can you imagine the incredible burden that is lifted off our shoulders when we realize the fallacy of these ideas? Can you imagine how Atlas felt when he was at long last able to set the world down?

When we finally choose to carry our burdens lightly, we will begin to shed these beliefs. In reality, we are *not* our creations, although we are incessantly creating. We also *cannot* achieve a nondisturbed state by gaining pleasure and avoiding pain. But we *can* get to a nondisturbed state, in the manner that God—and not the serpent—intended for us. We all have the possibility of achieving a nondisturbed state, and this is the goal of the resurrective path described in the following pages.

The fact that our beliefs create our experience means that the experiential world is the effect of our beliefs rather than the cause. And because we are the creators of our beliefs and, thereby, of the experiences that flow from them, we are the active source of our experiences and not the passive recipients of them. Moreover, what we create is quite distinct from ourselves as creators. Although I am writing this book, I am quite distinct from the created work. This book can be disposed of in many ways, yet I remain intact. I can give you this book, but that doesn't mean you hold me in your hands. Our slave mentality has led us to believe that we are what we create, that we *are* our body, our professional or family role, our social role, and so on. In fact, we identify with all of these at the same time. Yet none of these can be the "I" who knows each of these roles. To know something *always* implies a knower who, obviously, cannot be what he knows. The effect of our faulty education is to perpetuate the misperception that we are what we experience, that there is no "I" independent of the world of experience, that without attachment to the world of experience the "I" would cease to exist. But when we realize that quite the opposite is true, a door opens to our personal freedom.

The precedents for this view of reality come from the Old Testament, especially from two references in Genesis:

Then God said, "Let us make man in our own image and likeness." (Genesis 1:26)
So it was; and God saw all that He had made, and it was very good. (Genesis 1:31)

Being in the image and likeness of God means that we are able to carry out His work on earth. In fact, we do this all the time in that we are creating all the time, from the moment of our inception on this earth or even, some might say, from the moment of our conception.

Since we are made in God's image, we are *always* functioning *like* God. Moreover, we have been imbued with free will, which allows us to create destructive experiences as well as constructive ones. God's creation came as a consequence of an act of His will, a belief of His. His creation was *good*. We can continue to perpetuate the "good" and thereby sustain ourselves in God's likeness—His virtue—or we can impose our man-made creations upon His creation and thereby turn away from virtue. The impulses that drive us to impose our will upon God's remove us from our likeness to God. Such impulses serve the will to power, the will to hurt, the will to usurp the place of God, not the will to love.

The directives that serve as guideposts and beacons to take us through the wilderness of the world are the Ten Commandments. Every violation of these Commandments is directly related to the will to power, which *always* expresses itself through an individual often at the expense of someone else.

When God looked and saw that it was good, He knew that He wasn't His creation. His creation had to be separate from Him; otherwise, how could he look at it? Despite his detachment, He cared deeply about His creation, knowing that the beings He had created had to find their way back to Him. He loves those who love Him and weeps for those who do not. He knows they are the lost sheep, who have strayed and have been caught by the serpent.

Like God, we must detach ourselves from our creations, so that we stop mistaking ourselves for them. Absolutely nothing we create can ever lead us to God. We start returning to God only when we start detaching ourselves from our creations. A lack of detachment inevitably leads us to a grandiose vision of ourselves that in turn leads us to pain, suffering, and insuperable problems in our lives. We forget God by thinking that we are God.

The most valuable "thing" in this world is God, beside whom everything else pales in significance. We are here on this earth for one essential reason—to unite with Him. Everyone wants to return to Eden, to that nondisturbed state where life, health, and happiness are eternal. However, we have been misled by the serpent who promises us that we can get to the nondisturbed state by grasping at the temptations he puts in our way here on earth. And we believe the serpent in spite of the fact that no one has ever escaped death or unhappiness by fulfilling the desires engendered by those temptations. The serpent promises us immortality by making us believe we can become God. All of us have bitten the apple, and most of us continue to live hypnotized by the snake's deception, never achieving that promised eternal life.[3]

The belief that we can get to the nondisturbed state by gaining pleasure and avoiding pain is insidious because it seems natural to avoid pain. The serpent would have us believe that pain originates outside us and imposes itself on us by chance. In this scenario, pain is "bad," without intrinsic value, and should be avoided at all costs. But to reach Eden by the God road, we have to go through the pain that we encounter, for the pain is a reflection of what we have created for ourselves. Adopting a God-like perspective and acting in His image and likeness, we can look at our creation—in this instance, pain—and say what God said when He looked at His creation: "It is good." As we shall see later on, facing pain and seeing it as valuable can bring us to a nondisturbed state.

What we have been given as our birthright is control over our beliefs, over the creations of our mind. People, circumstances, experiences, events—in short, the experiential world—all belong to God. It is not given to us ever to have control over what happens in the experiential world—we cannot control the future and we cannot control how others behave. But we *can* control our beliefs. We can change our beliefs instantaneously. We can change our minds at will. Let us control what is ours to control and stop trying to control what is not ours to control.

Our power to control our own creations can shape a new course in life for each of us. For example, a student in one of my classes said that he had gone to see the Boston Symphony Orchestra at Carnegie Hall in New York City. Usually, at such concerts, he would get angry and feel like fighting with the people in the audience who fidget, turn pages, snore, and so on. On this occasion, however, he said to himself, "I created all these people and what they are doing, and I assume full responsibility for my creation." He said this without much expenditure of energy and in a peaceful manner, even with a feeling of lightness. Once he acknowledged his creation, the fidgeting, paper turning, and snoring ceased. Everyone, including himself, sat back and enjoyed the concert. That evening he fell asleep easily and had a peaceful, uninterrupted night's sleep. He said this was unusual because after a night at the concert with all its distractions, his reactive anger normally would stay with him long after the concert was over, and he would sleep fitfully.

Exercising this power is definitely as simple as that. The way to the truth is not as complicated as our miseducation would have us believe. As you read his story, can you grasp the power he felt in being able to shift an entire situation simply by shifting his belief? He didn't have to know why he had created the distractions to begin with—or, to be more technically correct, why he participated in the mutually shared beliefs that were manifesting as the experiences he described. No, he merely accepted his role in their creation, and everything changed for him in his world at that time.

If changing beliefs works as easily as this (try it for yourself), you can readily imagine why those institutions that function via the will to power (for instance, organized medicine, organized religion, and the military-industrial complex) and those that act on their behalf would not want you to possess this knowledge. These institutions educate us to believe that our experiences create who we are, that we are defined by the things that happen to us and over which we have no control and that we need these institutions to save us. Unpredictable forces "out there," we are led to believe, may harm or injure us by chance at any moment. Our recourse is to try to control the circumstances of our lives, but we can never directly control our circumstances, we cannot control our experiences or the actions of others. Yet we fully concentrate our efforts in this way, expending immense amounts of energy and wasting our physical and emotional resources. These futile efforts deplete us and move us into disease, degeneration, and death.

Our beliefs actually create experiences for us that have a particular purpose. The experiences mirror back to us the particular belief that we need to work on or master in our lives, either for our individual growth or for communal growth. We are here to learn from everything we create, for nothing happens by chance.

A patient came to me speaking of not feeling well, with symptoms of fatigue, swollen glands in her neck, and generalized achiness. Estelle had been given a diagnosis of Epstein-Barr syndrome, which is "caused" by a virus. She told me that she had difficulties in making friends and yearned to have more friends than the two who were currently in her life. She didn't really know how to account for her isolation other than through "bad luck," and she saw herself as personable, sociable, and friendly. Yet, because of her past experiences, she didn't think that she would be able to make more friends. Like all of us, she firmly subscribed to the proposition that her experiences created her beliefs, that what happened in the past clearly pointed to what would happen in the future.

This illusion had been perpetuated by a psychotherapist with whom Estelle had been in treatment for nearly fifteen years. After spending some time with her, I imparted to her my understanding that she herself had created the situation of having very few friends throughout her life. I pointed out that she rather enjoyed being reclusive for long periods so that she could develop her talents. Having many friends would have been an obstacle. In addition, she was hypercritical and a perfectionist, as hypercritical people tend to be. Her first impulse was to look for flaws in the people she met, and this way of relating, obviously, did not endear her to others. She considered what I said and agreed with my assessment, saying that pursuing the creative life required some sacrifice and that for her the sacrifice was intimacy in relationships. She could entertain people elegantly and graciously, but she didn't really want her contacts to go much further than a superficial dinner party or an evening get-together. It wasn't by chance that she was nearing forty and unmarried. After she realized that *she* had created the life she was leading, she asked, "What can I do to accept my role in all of this?" I answered that she should simply acknowledge the fact that she had created her situation and accept it *without* judgment, self-blame, self-criticism, self-flagellation, or any other critical response. This simple acceptance is a big first step to take, but she took it. And as she did so, her symptoms cleared up dramatically.

What happened to Estelle could happen to any of us who spend our lives living a mirage, an illusion that we ourselves have created. The objective of mind medicine is to keep us from making that mistake, to guard ourselves against the error of believing that experience creates belief, because the price we have to pay for that error is our emotional and physical health. The first step in spiritual medicine is to begin forgiving ourselves for making this mistake, so that we can begin to heal from it. This is exactly what happens when we acknowledge our role in creating what happens to us.

We may not know immediately which of our beliefs have generated what we encounter as an experience, but it is of inestimable benefit to recognize the process. Once this fact is acknowledged, we can try to figure out what belief we must have in order to engender the experience. Usually, the answer will come quickly, and then we can simply create a contrary belief that will manifest as a new and beneficial experience in our lives. In addition, we can push out the old belief. In mind medicine, one way to do this is through mental imagery, as in the following exercise:

Close your eyes and see the old belief written in the center of a blackboard. Wipe it away to the left with the left hand. Then write the new belief in the center of the blackboard and wipe it away to the right with the right hand. (For more such exercises, see Chapter 8.)

Later on, I will present other ways of removing old beliefs and creating new ones.

Another method of learning about our beliefs is to listen to the way we speak. We verbalize our beliefs incessantly, but without being aware of doing so. In my clinical work, I hear my patients' beliefs all the time. For example, suppose I give a patient the "homework" assignment of listening to his spoken beliefs, and the patient says, "That's going to be hard." That very statement reflects one of the patient's beliefs, and once the statement is made I know the homework won't be done because the belief will manifest as the experience of difficulty leading to frustration, to abandoning the task, and to coming in and saying the technique didn't work.

As these examples indicate, each of us creates a large number of personal beliefs that influence our lives. By thinking about our experiences and listening to ourselves speak, we can learn about our beliefs and see which are true and which false. A sure indication that a personal belief is false is that it refers to some standard—for example, the belief that you are supposed to be a good boy or girl.

Different people have different personal false beliefs, but in the course of my work I have noted twelve false beliefs that are so widely held that they are virtually universal. Each of us, men and women alike, has been so thoroughly indoctrinated in these beliefs that almost no one escapes their influence. I list these twelve "universal false beliefs" here and spell out their implications through the rest of this book.

Twelve Universally Held False Beliefs

1. There is chance.
2. Experience creates belief.
3. Death is inevitable.
4. Gravity works in a downward direction only.
5. Function follows form.
6. The purpose of living is to get to a nondisturbed state by gaining pleasure and avoiding pain.
7. Outside authorities know more about us than we know about ourselves.
8. It is important to be important so as to avoid inferiority.
9. It is important to be accepted so as to avoid rejection.
10. It is important to get attention so as to avoid neglect.
11. It is important to gain approval so as to avoid disapproval.
12. Truth and reality are the same.

Belief Systems and Children

I have been often asked, "What about children? Do they create their experience? Does a little infant with a serious illness create what happens to him? What about abused children?"

We create from the moment of birth till the moment of death—that is, creation is happening through us. At birth, our parents respond to us the moment they see our face. At that moment, infants experience their beliefs coming together with the beliefs of the adults charged with their care. When an infant or young child becomes ill, the child is being given the opportunity to learn something that he or she needs to know at that time, just as an adult who becomes ill is being offered a similar opportunity to learn. In the spiritual scheme of things, children and adults live under the same conditions of existence. In the case of childhood illness or even early death, it seems that the illness often brings some great transformation in the family dynamic. Families are brought together in a profoundly new way or are split apart by the event. The true relationships within the family come to light. Whatever the outcome, healing is brought to the family, either as union or harmony or as an end to the unacknowledged suffering that preceded the breakup. In the end, the child's work may be done, and he or she bids adieu to this present life circumstance.

As for child abuse, it has been a fact of life for millennia. *Child murder and child abuse are among the oldest known crimes.* To understand child abuse, we need to look at it from the mind medicine viewpoint, which is quite different from the viewpoint of currently established psychology.

When Freud first investigated the workings of the mind, he encountered many women who revealed to him shocking stories of sexual abuse at the hands of their close relatives. At first, he believed these stories, but as he developed his psychoanalytic theories he came to a different conclusion. Freud's theory depended upon the proposition that what motivates the individual is an unconscious fantasy of wanting, as a child, to eliminate the parent of the same sex in order to possess the parent of the opposite sex. This formulation is known as the Oedipus complex, and it is a cornerstone of psychoanalytic thinking. Thus, Freud came to believe that the sexual abuse recounted by his women patients had not actually happened but had been fantasized. To Freud, the stories were constructions that exemplified the underlying unconscious desire, the Oedipus complex. But in recent years so many people have bravely come forward with painful revelations of childhood sexual abuse that we are now witnessing a dramatic anti-Freudian reaction. Instead of doubting and disbelieving the victims of child abuse, we are springing to their defense. And this acceptance of abuse as a reality of life has spawned a new psychology of what causes emotional trouble.

This apparent reversal, however, contains a hidden irony. Both the Freudian and anti-Freudian perspectives are based on the premise that experience creates belief—that is, the experiences of childhood determine what we become in adult life. This perspective has never been proven and never can be proven, for it is one of the most devastating false beliefs held today. It has contributed to the criminality and drug taking that pervades American life by giving criminals and other abusers a convenient rationalization: "I'm not responsible for my behavior. Look at what happened to me in my childhood and what my parents and others did to me. It's what happened then that makes me behave like this now. All my actions are prompted by unconscious urges over which I have no control and for which I can't be held responsible." Even worse, society accepts and condones this behavior on the same grounds: "Look where he grew up." "He was beaten as a child. How else would you expect him to grow up?" "He came from a deprived home so he behaves this way." "He didn't get real love at home, only material things, so he had to resort to drugs." On and on go the rationalizations for moral errors that have offended and injured others, sometimes to a hideous degree.

We cannot ask why a child would choose to create harmful beliefs and the consequent painful experiences.

"Why" is an excellent question when asked by scientists interested in the physical world, but it is not relevant in the area of human relations. "Why" only provokes us to create stories, explanations that turn into burdensome false beliefs. When we stop asking why, we will stop blaming ourselves and others and stop hanging on to the past.

A final point needs to be made about established psychology—namely, its tendency to blame parents for the moral errors of their offspring. This process of blaming parents prevents us from carrying out the Fifth Commandment: "Honor thy father and mother so that thy days may be long" (Exodus 20:12). (Note the implied promise of longevity.)

Accepting the spiritual point of view gives us a true and absolute understanding of such apparently tragic events as childhood illness and child abuse. For spiritual reality encompasses reincarnation, which means that when our physical body ceases to function, the soul that is housed in it is released. At some later time, this soul will engage a new body and will be escorted by an angel back to earth, where it selects its new womb opening, its new parents. But when it comes back, it carries all its dispositions from earlier incarnations, all its significant beliefs, which now have to be played out in its current life. The new baby has to face the experiences engendered by the beliefs brought from its previous existence.

This understanding throws a whole new light on coping with childhood illness, by changing our sadness to acceptance and love. This may be difficult to believe, especially for those of you who are new to spiritual life or who remain in the antispiritual stance of skepticism. Remember, *it can only be true for you if you have experi-*

mented with it or experienced it directly. Blind faith is as injurious as reflexive skepticism. To accept what I say as true without making your own discovery flies in the face of the First and Second Commandments and stands against movement in the direction of freedom. How these commandments turn us toward freedom is the subject of the next chapter.

3

The Moral Shield

The Lord is my strength and my shield; my heart
trusted in him, and I am helped.

—Psalm 28:7

About four thousand years ago, the Chinese made
a significant contribution to our understanding of the
origin of illness. They said that illness enters us from the
outside. They called the cause of illness "external per-
nicious influences." Unless internal circumstances threw
the person into a state of imbalance, however, the influences would not be able to enter and disturb the natural
equilibrium.

In the West, a corresponding viewpoint in the ancient medical tradition was that all disease came about
through possession by external demonic influences.
These forces could not enter without an inner emotional
or physical imbalance created by moral errors. One

could not expect to act in error without repercussions that would be felt emotionally and physically and subsequently manifested as possession.

The modern equivalents to demonic possession in conventional medicine are microorganisms such as bacteria, fungi, and viruses. On the emotional level, in conventional psychology, the equivalents are obsessive thinking, compulsive behavior, and phobia. We become ill through creating an inner disturbance on all levels of our being, which sets us up for invasive illness.

In spiritual medicine, the key to internal stability or instability lies in our moral actions. Morality holds a preeminent position in Western spirituality. Unlike Eastern thought, which makes the mind the starting point for truth and reality, Western thought makes the world the starting point. In the East, the world is considered illusionary, wholly a structure of the mind, and the fundamental spiritual error is a cognitive perceptual one, a mistaking of our little ego self for the true Self. The Eastern aim is to correct this cognitive error by divorcing the little ego self from the true Self by the exercise of compassion, not love.

For the West, the fundamental spiritual error is a moral one—the desire to become God and usurp God's knowledge and power for ourselves. We correct this moral error by marrying our will to God's will, by restraining our will instead of letting it run rampant. It is our relationship to the world, to that which appears to be exterior to us, that becomes crucial in our effort to join our will with that of God. Love is the force ordering our moral relationship to the world, including other people. Acting morally requires that we love, and love requires the presence of two: the lover and the loved one, or the individual and the world. Western spirituality is based on duality, the number two. The higher transformation of this twoness occurs via love and truth. The lower degeneration of twoness that leads to decay is manifested through doubt, which is the root cause of all illness and death.

Whenever we speak of our relationship to the world or the relationship of the lover to the loved one, we are automatically connected to a moral reality. Moral reality is the world God created, as described in the first chapter of Genesis. We have been born into a world of truth, love, and moral reality. Morality *is* truth, love, and absolute good. We are born with free will and a mandate to preserve the moral beauty with which we have been bequeathed. This injunction is stated in the second chapter of Genesis, where we are told that the "Lord took man and placed him in the Garden to tend and keep it" (Genesis 2:15). To the extent that we do not follow this injunction, we scar and deface this beautiful organism called earth. At the same time that we deface the world, we disfigure our own beautiful organism.

If we ignore the existence of the vertical, spiritual reality and acknowledge the material reality of horizontal causality alone, we shall be doomed to go on disfiguring and defacing our earth. For instance, in the horizontal realm of the physical world environmental pollutants contribute to the rise of cancer. Although this is a direct cause-and-effect relationship, the meta-cause is in the vertical realm. Events in the physical world are only the final common pathway of the thoughts and deeds of humans. In this example, the question is, What has created the environmental breakdown and pollution's cancerous consequences? The answer is the greed, rapacity, and avarice that now run amok in the world. The Tenth Commandment speaks to this very point by urging us to shun these sins. Our unchecked exploitation of the earth and the runaway social and moral madness of society are mirrored by the scourge of cancer, the physical version of our out-of-balance social conditions. Cancer—hyperindividualistic and unchecked—dominates its environment and eventually destroys its host. And like cancer on the microlevel, we on the macrolevel are overrunning our environment and destroying our host—the earth.

It is interesting to note that this raping of the planet has been rationalized by a statement made in the Bible: that man shall have *dominion* over nature. Over the past four to five centuries the word *dominion* has been conveniently understood in the West as meaning "ownership." It is correct, however, to define the term *dominion* as synonymous with the term *stewardship*. As stewards we should protect and care for our environment and treat our planet as a living organism that sustains our lives and perpetuates the common good.

On a global scale, we are surrounded by an atmospheric shield called the ozone layer, which protects us from an excess of the sun's ultraviolet rays. On a subatomic-physical level, we humans have a shield of light surrounding us that has been variously called an aura (by those involved with the psychic sciences) and an electromagnetic field (by those involved with the natural sciences). Natural scientists estimate that this electromagnetic field extends out to a distance of about 36 inches from our physical surface. While psychic scientists say that the aura extends much farther, both groups would agree that the macrocosm and microcosm are analogous: as above (the protective ozone layer of the atmosphere), so below (the aura or electromagnetic field shielding each of us).

We can take the notion of protection one step further and speak about a mental shield also—our moral life. So from the outside in, we have three shields: the ozone layer, the auric or electromagnetic shield, and the moral shield. One of our great tasks in this life is to prevent any of these shields from being pierced. On the macrocosmic level, we are in trouble because pollutants have caused holes to appear in the ozone layer, permitting dangerous levels of ultraviolet radiation to penetrate to the earth's surface. On the physical level, the drastic rise in cancer rates indicates that our auric or electromagnetic shield is also being pierced. And the destruction of our moral shield is reflected in the fact that mental aberrations have led in this century to mass death on a scale beyond anything in the history of the world.

Piercing any of these shields opens the door to destructive forces. The ancient wisdom of the West has always enjoined us to build a moral shield around ourselves to prevent the deadly forces of evil and disease from entering. Each breach of our moral shield creates a port of entry for destructive forces. But when we act in accordance with our moral precepts, as they come to us through the invisible, spiritual reality, we strengthen our shields, perpetuating both our own life and the life of the planet.

So, to heal the planet we must begin to heal ourselves, to correct our own moral errors, which have led directly to the calamities that beset us. The greatest moral error, that of wanting to usurp the knowledge and power of God, lies at the heart of all the ailments that plague the world today. Currently, we are absolutely asleep to the enormity of this danger, but we can still save ourselves and our planet. In effect, God has told humanity: "I have made and destroyed many worlds. This one I have made. It is up to you to preserve or destroy it. I have given you free will and choice in this matter. The final outcome is in your hands."

The God-created world is a moral world based on truth, freedom, and love, the three essential ingredients in morality and in beneficial human relationships. The man-made world, the one we have grafted onto the God-created world, is based not on morality but on power and on perpetuating the false belief that the purpose of living is to attain a nondisturbed state by gaining pleasure and avoiding pain.

What is the real purpose of living? The answer is that we are here to discover truth, to get past the lie that the serpent told to Adam and Eve. That lie was a monumental moral test put in their way by God, and we, too, are being tested morally. Falsehoods are put in our way continually, lies that we ourselves create to define our personal reality. These lies lead us to succumb to the corruption placed in our path, and in doing so we have disfigured ourselves and our planet. Our purpose is to find our way through this morass of misinformation and, by discovering the truth, begin to make the correct moral choices that will heal these disfigurements.

We are made in the image and likeness of God, as told to us at the beginning of the book of Genesis. *Image* means that we bear the seed within us to become immortal. *Likeness* means that we are born with God's virtue, morality, and truth.

The fundamental error at the heart of our disfigurement is our attempt to usurp the knowledge and power of God, to become God. We attempt this usurpation in many ways.

God in His infinite mercy has given us the ability to make corrections. We have been put on earth to remember our likeness to God and to maintain and cultivate that likeness in order to serve God. We have the option of not remembering God, an option that we have been exercising all too extensively.

God already commanded us on how to behave in the Ten Commandments. These precepts, delivered by Moses and reiterated by Jesus in the Sermon on the Mount, contain an absolute moral code to which we must adhere if we are to preserve ourselves, prevent illness and death, and save this planet.

Exodus 15:26 provides a clear statement of the relationship between moral life and health. In this verse God *promises* the Israelites freedom from disease if they carry out these precepts—precepts upon which mind medicine draws. Exodus 15:26 says: "And [God] said, If thou wilt diligently hearken to the voice of the LORD thy God, and wilt do that which is right in his sight, and wilt give ear to his commandments, and keep all his statutes, I will put none of these diseases upon thee, which I have brought upon the Egyptians: for I *am* the LORD that healeth thee."

Our task is to enact these precepts first in mind and then in physical life. Our thoughts are progenitors of our actions. We have been put in this Garden to tend, maintain, and cultivate our own individual gardens of reality. Some of the seeds we plant will bear nutritious fruit, while others will bear inedible growths that could poison us. What germinates depends on our moral thoughts, feelings, and actions. The choice is always ours.

What we create through these inner seeds will manifest to our perception in the external world. What is born in the inner forum of our consciousness—the beliefs, images, and feelings (themselves beliefs and images)—will take shape in the world and be reflected back to us as our experiences. In order to make use of this knowledge, we must not be deceived into thinking that our personal experiences exist independent of us, outside of us, having nothing to do with us, until they affect us, "causing" us to respond to them. Our moral being, whatever its state, will be reflected in the kinds of experiences we have. If we lie to ourselves and others, if we cheat, steal, are envious, jealous, or angry or behave in any other morally askew way, sooner or later we will suffer a consequence injurious to our overall being. The consequences are experiences that ask us to correct whatever error we are committing. If we don't change, we constantly repeat these errors and constantly experience the consequences, and as the accumulation builds up, our moral shield is weakened and our exposure to illness becomes greater and greater—until finally we succumb.

Carrying out the commandments poses for us the challenge of becoming ever watchful of our thoughts and actions. The fabric of all life's situations is tied to the commandments, in that there is no social interaction or relational interchange that does not have some connection to one or more of the commandments. They cover every possible situation that can arise in our lives. Being aware of the presence and operation of the commandments in ourselves is the core therapeutic practice of mind medicine. It is the only treatment we have for our ills.

Moreover, we have to become aware of the subtleties of each of the commandments. When we hastily criticize our children in front of others, we are murdering them. When we say "I'll take care of it tomorrow," we are bearing false witness if we do not do it. When we feel anxious and worried about the future, we are making a graven image—a conclusion about the future—and at the same time bearing false witness. When we push ahead of someone in line at the supermarket, we are coveting. When we speak ill of our parents to someone else, we are clearly not honoring our father and mother. When we shop in stores seven days a week, we are not remembering the Sabbath—a day set aside to reverse our habitual activities.

Gossip columnists in newspapers around the country make their living bearing false witness. Money, status, and power are worshipped and revered, instead of the invisible, spiritual reality. Competitiveness is rewarded overwhelmingly. Cocaine and heroin rob our souls and weaken our character and physical constitution. Mixing two things together—drinking and driving, for example—is an act of adultery.

All spiritual disciplines teach that our lives would be substantially different if we heeded our own actions in a conscious, watchful way. It requires an act of our intentional will to put a brake on our habitual behavior and see how our actions reflect or disturb the image of God, our moral image.

We are not generally taught about the consequences of our actions. If we do not understand that every thought and action has a consequence, not only for ourselves but for society as well, we have no reason to consider our behavior. Most of the consequences of our actions are unintended.[1] It is unlikely, then, that we would be able to see that illness is an unintended consequence of erroneous behavior.

The Commandments and Daily Life

In the Western spiritual tradition, our earthly lives are judged in a heavenly court as to whether we will be given the grace to continue in this life. This heavenly court is convened for every one of us. In the Jewish tradition, its earthly counterpart occurs on Yom Kippur, the Day of Atonement, when the Book of Life is opened and every penitent hopes to be inscribed for another year of life.

The truth is that we do not have to know in advance the consequences of our actions. It is not in our hands to know them. They lie in the future, which is not our realm of knowledge. All we need to know is that our thoughts and actions do have consequences. The holy men of India name these consequences "karma." Throughout our lives, we are always free to believe or not believe in the connection between the commandments and our health.

Not only are the commandments prescriptions for a healing, sane life, they are also detoxifying agents. In the next section I will try to give some relevant examples of the operation of these ten precepts in our daily lives. Think of this section as an opportunity to look at your life situation, to explore the commandments that are most relevant to your experiences, and to begin to correct your errors. Keep in mind that you should not judge or condemn yourself for what you discover. Do not criticize or flagellate yourself if you forget to do this practice or delay doing it. All judgments, criticisms, and condemnations are lies; they are part of bearing false witness and making graven images against yourself. Making corrections means acknowledging the presence of the invisible reality, of reconnecting with and returning to the source out of which we all come. Returning and connecting are the source of salvation in all Western spiritual and religious traditions. Returning to God fulfills being born in the image and likeness of God. At the same time, it fulfills the First Commandment: to put no other god before God. There is no god but God. Nothing need obscure that vision in the invisible reality.

The First Commandment

The First Commandment says that we are not to worship any visible reality, to the detriment of our awe and reverence of the invisible reality. Nothing in the visible world can match the worth, mystery, power, and lovingness of God. Immense forces in this world are arrayed around us to persuade us to the contrary. The choice to return to this belief and practice is an essential one for human existence. Our constant need to choose between life and death, good and evil, love and power, is our purpose for being alive. Our lives proceed from the tension between ceaseless calls to choose life or death. Our choice sets in motion either constructive or destructive consequences.

No one is exempt from having to choose—not the most desperate criminal, and not the most exalted saint. Our choice is determined by the beliefs we have brought into this life and by those that family, friends, and educators inculcated in us as children. Our worldview—our fundamental beliefs about life—is essentially in place by the time we are seven or eight years old. Later, we embrace new beliefs that accord with our own and reject those that do not fit with them. Contrary to what we may think, we are not really open to the new, and as we age, we become more and more inflexible, holding on to fixed beliefs and rejecting any change at all.

Paradoxically, this rigidity makes us more and more dependent on our culture to confirm our attitudes. We then become more susceptible to cultural beliefs. The reason for this susceptibility is that we don't want to lose the support of those around us, believing that they make our lives more pleasurable and consequently less painful, investing them with authority and power over us and the ability to judge us and decide our fate.

As we think and believe more habitually, we replace our connection with the invisible reality with something directly tangible: We replace God with man, substituting faith in the visible for faith in the invisible.

Have you or anyone you know ever waited on line overnight to get a ticket to see Frank Sinatra, Elvis Presley, Michael Jackson, Madonna, or Bruce Springsteen? Perhaps you know someone who paid an extraordinary amount of money to see Michael Jordan play basketball. If so, that person (or you yourself) made an error with respect to the First Commandment.

Many men and women expend too much energy on other people or objects that promise to bring them pleasure or respite from pain. When the false illusions about these things have passed, the returned pain necessitates another round of wasted energy on the pursuit of relief or pleasure. The perpetuation of such cyclic behavior is addiction. We become addicted to the display of the things that parade endlessly before our eyes.

Don't put any god before God. Don't obscure your view of God or access to him. Call on the invisible reality anytime you choose. All you need to do is offer a prayer, in the form of quietly thinking about or feeling for God. You can ask for forgiveness or guidance. You can ask for things in an indirect way ("Please show me a way to heal myself," rather than "please heal me"). Prayer can also be offered through mental imagery, or concretized prayer—prayer given form. (Chapter 7 contains numerous imagery and prayerlike exercises for healing.)

The Second Commandment

The Second Commandment states that we are not to create graven images, or erect and bow down before idols. The difficulties in keeping this commandment alone can account for most of the troubles we suffer.

Making a graven image means to create a physical representation by hand or a mental one by mind. Examples of mental graven images are conclusions, explanations, if-then thoughts, expectations, predictions, fixed beliefs, and any thought process that projects us into the future or into the past. We spend most of our waking lives engaged in graven-image making.

Mental graven images are *always* pieces of false information. Since they are about the future, they have no truth value. Yet we act on those bits of erroneous data—and suffer detrimental consequences. In the Bible this activity was called making a "golden calf," when material life was revered more than spiritual life.

Acts of idolatry cast other people in roles of special importance or authority, like doctors, movie stars, sports stars, clergymen, and politicians. Other acts of idolatry attribute power to things and pursuits—for example, to money, power, fame.

Duress, intimidation, and even threats of violence and murder demand that we give away power. The pressures on us to surrender our authority are enormous and omnipresent. It takes a lot of will to resist them, especially if we accept the belief-system that external authorities know more than we do and that personal material acquisition is the ultimate purpose of life.

The thrust of education supports beliefs that run absolutely contrary to the Second Commandment, bowing to experts and authorities, trusting in them. Possibly we need to refer to authorities in evaluating the quality of objects or services we use. But when it comes to our life and relationships, no one is more authoritative than we ourselves are. If we allow our miseducation to continue to fool us, we will bow down before a statue of Baal in some form. The notion that we must subject ourselves to the supposed expertise of an authority is a deception of no small proportions. It may be quite valuable for us to have mentors who encourage our freedom, but not tormentors who would take our freedom away.

As I have mentioned, the difficulties in keeping this commandment are enormous. We need to be watchful whenever we come in contact with someone who presents himself or herself as an authority. In the context of health, we need to change our overreliance on doctors. It is a pervasive cultural belief today that doctors have *the* answers to questions of illness and health, life and death. By persisting in holding this belief, we opt to depend on someone else for our health and life. Instead, we need to rely on our own judgment and authority by listening to the inner voice of truth that speaks to us in the present tense and an imperative voice.

A clinical instance illustrates the Second Commandment:

Sarah, a highly successful woman, had gone through some rough times. She had made and lost a fortune over the years. When I saw her, she had rallied back from difficult circumstances and was on the brink of a financial breakthrough with a number of projects that she had been nurturing simultaneously. As this breakthrough was about to happen, Sarah received a job offer in a completely unrelated field, one that would put her in the public eye. The offer was very attractive and she felt quite tempted to take it. She asked a number of people close to her for their opinion about what her decision should be. She came to see me in a frazzled state, having heard many different perspectives.

We did the imagery exercise from Chapter 2 ("Finding the Room of Silence") in which she saw herself in a room standing in front of the anxiety. She then turned her back on the anxiety and went through a door into another room and through a door in that room to another room. As she went on, she related that she had been calling person after person, asking for advice and becoming increasingly unnerved when they gave it to her. Finally she found her room of silence, which she could calmly explore as she wished to find her own answer.

As Sarah was a spiritually oriented person, I set her predicament within the framework of the commandments. She was clearly seeking an outside authority to tell her right from wrong. She complained that she was feeling alone and needed the help of others. I explained to her that whenever we turn from the invisible reality, we feel alone. For the invisible reality, Sarah had substituted the visible reality—in the form of her many advisers. There was little value, I said, in putting the visible reality in between herself and the invisible.

She said that made a lot of sense, since she had been seeking answers from outside rather than from within herself. She was shortchanging and ultimately sabotaging herself by shifting her own authority to others. By surrendering her power, she had let herself be deflected from her creative pursuits. Along with this new understanding of her own efficacy came a sense of new-found power and relief from anxiety. She turned down the job offer and completed the work that was where her heart really was. Since then, whenever anxiety has come back to her, she has been easily able to calm herself by using this imagery exercise.

Sarah's dilemma is no different from those we all face in our lives. Almost all of us abdicate our power and turn to outside authorities. You might object here that a doctor has more training than you do in the body or a particular illness, so you must turn to this authority to get the definitive word about what you should do. It is certainly possible that a doctor knows something about an illness, but he or she is by no means a greater authority about you than you are. At best a doctor can offer you an opinion (couched all too often as fact). Only we can truly know what's best for us.

The Third Commandment

The Third Commandment says that we are not to take God's name in vain. This means that we must not represent ourselves as something we are not, nor idly invoke the invisible reality when it suits our convenience, nor mislead other people, nor achieve personal gain from invoking the invisible reality when we don't believe in it or its truth.

Using God's name in vain has been a longstanding historical source of pain and prejudice. God has been invoked to account for the superiority of one person over another and to legitimize acts of war. The Islamic world calls for waging a *jihad*, or holy war, to remove or convert those who do not accept the superiority of Allah. Nazism was a "holy war" waged to wipe out Jews, Catholics, and ultimately God from the face of the earth. All major wars since biblical times have probably been holy wars fought in the name of some religious institution that presumed that God was on its side and that shed blood and subjected others in the name of God, as though that which is endlessly creative and life-giving would condone and support the spilling of blood. The implication is that God's purpose is to put everyone into captivity and enslavement or else kill them. If that is the case, then why does God clearly state in Deuteronomy, "Choose life"?

To avoid taking God's name in vain, we must ask ourselves whom our actions are serving. Are you motivated by love of power, or by the power of love? Are you being harmless, considerate, and contributing to your family and the world?[2] We have to be frank and honest with ourselves. If you build your life on a false foundation, sooner or later it will come tumbling down.

The Fourth Commandment

The Fourth Commandment speaks to remembering the Sabbath. The Sabbath is a day of rest that we set aside when we remember that He who created us rested after His work was completed. Thus do we emulate God and remember our connection with Him. The great healing key embedded into the Sabbath is what my teacher Madame Muscat calls "reversing." Reversing means turning around, or doing the opposite. Observing the Sabbath impels us to do things we normally don't do, or disengage from what we do every day. By remembering and resting, we reverse our habitual daily life. The general health and well-being of our society suffers because most Americans do not observe a Sabbath. Today there is no rest from commerce, no pause for our daily lives. The impetus to rush is fostered everywhere. But rest is essential to healing, and the Sabbath is an excellent way to "practice" rest. In observing the Sabbath, we are returning our thoughts to the present, away from the past or future.

During the Sabbath we can not only center and balance ourselves but undergo transformation. Our society is not arranged to make Sabbath living easy, but even though its demands pull us away from rest, you can make it a day of great play—especially if your week has been all work. The Sabbath was made for us to restore vitality and meaning into our lives.

The Fifth Commandment

The Fifth Commandment says to honor your father and mother and in so doing gain long life. To honor parents is to respect them. You do not have to love them. They decided to bear you and give you a chance to be on this earth and thereby give you the opportunity to find freedom and enlightenment.

Children tend to personalize the problems of their parents and believe themselves to be singled out for unwarranted punishment. Modern psychology has created the impression that parents victimize their children and thereby create some sort of lasting disturbance. But not even our suffering outweighs the miracle of being born, giving us the opportunity to find our self-realization. We should focus not on what our parents did or didn't do to us but on living out the precepts, our first order of business.

By disparaging and blaming our parents, we move against the perpetuation and continuity of life. We cannot sit in judgment of them, just as we would not want our children to sit in judgment of us. Blaming others often diverts us from learning our own lessons, sorting through our pain, and getting on with our lives.

The breakup of the family is one of the glaring problems of American life. It is especially problematic because the pressures that have sundered families and turned family members against each other are insidious. These pressures include psychology; large corporations that shift family members away from each other; biases against minorities and their impoverishment, resulting in many single-parent families; the drug culture, in which heavy indulgence in addictive substances creates soulless people without love, compassion, or humanity.

The religious, ethical, and spiritual impulses that educate us to love, honor, obey, share, and care for ourselves and others foster family cohesion and parental respect. But these impulses have all too often been submerged by the tidal wave of commercial and corporate greed and the idolization of money. Spiritual values are absent from American life, as well as almost everywhere else, and we need to rediscover our individual balance, a higher purpose to save ourselves and each other.

When you find yourself berating or bad-mouthing your parents, remember that whatever you have achieved here, you could not have done without your parents' decision to put you here. There are no accidents in spiritual life. There are no unplanned or accidental births. You were not born here by chance, but by choice. We all need to thank our parents for giving us our opportunities of life.

Abused children, like everyone else, have something to learn from working to respect their parents. They can help us as a society understand the pervasive and powerful murderous impulse that dominates our world today. Parents are fully responsible for their behavior and have accountability, and we have no obligation to love them, only to honor them. But without honoring them, we perpetuate abusive behavior in our own lives.

In our era we have the first real possibility in recorded history to transform violence into love. The prophet Isaiah said that we will beat our swords into plowshares; the lion will lie down with the lamb; we shall not know war anymore. That prophecy may yet come to pass, and we may well stand on the brink of it.

In sum: Honoring father and mother perpetuates tradition, life on a societal level, and individual life. At the same time, it prevents violent, murderous behavior, as we recognize that all human beings are to be respected as honored family members.

The Sixth Commandment

The Sixth Commandment says that we are not to commit murder. There are many forms of murder besides physical murder, forms that in the ancient tradition were considered to be on a par with it. There were three such types: not giving credit to your sources, to people who helped you or whose creations inspired you; humiliating someone in public; and depression. Not giving credit murders a person in name. Humiliating someone murders a person in character. Depression means self-murder.

Depression is an almost ubiquitous emotional state in our day, so it is worth taking a long look at it. Depression has various gradations and many different elements. Essentially, a depressed person has turned away from the present to the past, leaving life. Depression is a living death. We have accepted that dimension of our existence that is dead, finished, gone, buried, done.

The story of Lot's wife neatly illustrates the dangers of "looking back." When Lot and his wife escaped Sodom and Gomorrah, the land of injustice and hedonism, they were told not to look back from where they had come. Lot's wife did not heed this directive and looked back, whereupon she was turned into a pillar of salt. As she looked back to what she was losing and giving up, she experienced great regret about her past and began to cry. She became covered with salt from the tears of regret, and when this salt eventually hardened, she became a pillar of salt.

Similarly, when we become filled with salt, our arteries harden and we become sclerotic, or hardened and rigid. In sclerosis, we lose flexibility and malleability, as in the process of aging. When we look back, we regret, cry, and sclerose—become hardened and rigid—setting the stage for our demise. Every story associated with depression is just a story, with no truth value, as illusory as a story about the future. To account for our suffering now, we create still another story—an instance of experience creating belief, an opportunity to blame circumstances.

We always seem to think that our circumstances determine our inner state. Yet we are in charge of our inner state and have the capacity to create our own circumstances. Our beliefs create our experiences, rather than the other way around. To give up depression, you need to give up the past, to relinquish the grip of the guilt feelings it engenders. Whatever event that disturbed you is gone. If you are still making errors as a result, these errors need to be corrected.

The tools presented in this book are intended to correct errors. In accepting these tools, you are accepting responsibility for the errors and seeking remedies for them. In making a correction, you are automatically forgiving yourself. You need no intermediary to grant you absolution or forgiveness. You need forgiveness only from those whom you have harmed by your errors. At first, you recognize and admit your errors—confess them to yourself, as it were, to your heart. Ask yourself or God for forgiveness. Then ask those whom you have injured for their forgiveness. In that way you cleanse yourself of whatever darkness you have brought.

David, a man who was quite successful in his worldly life, came to see me because of serious eye problems. He had atrophy of the left optic nerve and lens deformation of the right eye. His physician had told him that his condition was incurable. He was attuned to the spiritual aspect of life, however, and had some inkling that his blindness was connected to some error in his spiritual life. He came to me seeking mental imagery work.

As is customary in the practice of spiritual medicine, I asked David about the circumstances surrounding his vision loss. What was he not seeing? What did he not want to look at? Was he suffering any guilt feeling? (Remember that Oedipus, the legendary Greek king, blinded himself out of guilt for committing a moral error.) David was decidedly intent on healing himself and was eager to uncover intimate and sometimes morally unpleasant details of his life. These details became important elements in the successful treatment.

Our educative-therapeutic work consisted of David's making corrections for his moral indiscretions, along with practicing specific imagery exercises to restore his vision. The imagery exercises had him clean out his eyes, take in air through his pupils to move the aqueous fluid properly, and cleanse his lenses; a sanctified being (in his case, Jesus Christ) would spit in his eyes to enhance healing. David physically bathed his eyes in healing water that he obtained from a religious healing center in North America (analogous to Lourdes in France). He made restitution to all those whom he had wronged, wherever he could. This restitution was usually in monetary form, forgiving the debts of those who owed him and maintaining a generous attitude in the face of all this forfeiture. David, a naturally generous man, was financially able to carry out these actions. He was able to make the corrections rather easily and without resentment since he knew he was making them for his own self-healing. He received back an unanticipated outpouring of love from those to whom he made restitution, including two ex-wives and a relative whose $75,000 debt he forgave. At the end of six months, David's vision began to improve. At the end of a year his vision was restored so that he could work normally and was able to drive his car again. This healing has lasted three years, as of the writing of this book.

The Seventh Commandment

The Seventh Commandment says, "Do not commit adultery." The very obvious form of adultery is a marital partner who takes up an affair with a third party. Adultery may be the single most destructive factor that contributes to the dissolution of the family structure. The presence of the third party hangs like a shadowy specter over a marriage and family, like the serpent in the Garden with Adam, Eve, and God. God said to Eve, "Be faithful to the one voice, to the voice of One." The third party—the serpent—asked the couple to renounce this faithfulness. Every act of adultery is a reenactment of that Edenic act of faithlessness. Marriage is (among other things) a stage upon which we can practice being faithful to one person—and to the One.

Some cultures, it is true, have institutionalized adultery as a cultural norm. We may try to justify adulterous acts by saying we need outlets and succor from another person to offset the pain of our present circumstances, but these rationalizations legitimize a fundamentally hedonistic impulse. The word *adultery* means "to weaken," and any adulterous act weakens the situation in which it occurs. It is an error with respect both to our integrity and to our relationship with the invisible reality.

Adultery produces weakening through the act of mixing two things that essentially don't belong together—like business and pleasure—in the same pot. The Book of Deuteronomy clearly and concisely gives four cautions against this mixing: "don't plant two different seeds in the same field," "don't put an ox and an ass on the same plow," "don't mix linen and silk together," and "don't mix milk and meat." These cautionary statements suggest how we should handle fundamental relationships in life. For example, we should pay attention to what foods we eat together, for eating those that don't belong together—like milk and meat—may create serious digestive disturbances. Milk and meat independently take a long time to digest, putting a burden on the digestive tract. Taken together, the burden they place on the intestinal tract becomes proportionally greater.

The Eighth Commandment

The Eighth Commandment says, "Do not steal." We are all familiar with physical stealing, but we may not realize that stealing can happen on other levels as well: emotional and social. Let us say we make arrangements to meet each other at the movie theater at eight o'clock. I am there at eight, but you don't come until nine. You tell me that a telephone call came just before you were to leave the house and you lost track of the time. Regardless of that excuse you have effectively stolen one hour of time from me. In my practice I hear very often about time wasted by false promises of an early marriage, or an impending divorce, or any number of variants. Time stolen is irretrievable. We must be careful not to steal others' time, nor allow our time to be stolen from us.

As I mentioned under the Sixth Commandment, not giving credit to one's sources is a form of murder. It is also a form of stealing—stealing the spotlight, name, and fame that may come from somebody else's idea or invention.

Among the illnesses encountered most frequently in my practice are those engendered when family members are cheated out of their inheritance or are victims of deceit or the withholding of money due them by other family members. In these instances, I encourage the cheated person actively to pursue legal action against their family if possible. At first, they usually show a great deal of resistance to this recourse, but when it becomes clear to them that there is no family loyalty or love, they accept the idea. The health-giving effects of such legal action cannot be emphasized enough. In a number of instances, family culprits who owned up to their deviance and made restitution have experienced healthful effects.

The Ninth Commandment

The Ninth Commandment says, "Do not bear false witness." False witness includes gossiping, spreading rumors, lying, slander, libel, saying something that is true but that shouldn't be said, saying something that is not true but shouldn't be said, and not saying something that needs to be said.

The ubiquity of lying is apparent to everyone. We have all been exposed to it in our personal life, in social situations, and on the political level, and we have all felt its consequences.

For example, a young woman named Leah came to see me with physical and emotional problems that were preventing her from functioning properly. A gifted person, she had overcome poverty and family abandonment early in life to marry, raise a family, run a hugely successful business, and then enter a second successful career as a health professional. About six months before she came to see me, while she was on vacation in a foreign country, serious episodes of panic began to come over her. She had to be flown back to the United States and was thereafter frightened to venture out of her house alone. She could not travel any appreciable distance on her own without accompaniment. Not only did she become frightened and confused, she began to suffer from lower abdominal pain. Her physical exam and laboratory work-up revealed no physical pathology.

In our work together, which addressed her moral relatedness, Leah discovered that she had been persistently and continuously lying, bearing false witness. She embarked on a course of consciously not bearing false witness, to correct this tendency and to be forthright with herself and others. She knew that by putting herself in order on the moral level, she would put herself in order emotionally and physically. She very quickly found herself feeling much better, and her panic disappeared.

Leah discovered that she harbored a great deal of anger and resentment against her husband. (He had been with her on the trip.) As she became thoroughly honest, she took charge of her life, grew more self-confident, enhanced her sense of real self, became thoroughly relaxed, and really enjoyed life more than she ever had. It was wonderful to watch her healing over a three-month period as it progressed from the moral to the emotional and then physical levels.

Her change in consciousness had a ripple effect on her family and friends, permitting them to become more focused and centered in their own lives. This development is not unusual. As Moses, Jesus, and Buddha aligned or centered their consciousness, they created a similar shift in consciousness in those around them. I have often found the same phenomenon in my patients and their family setting.

Lying often takes very subtle forms. It is so natural to say "I'll call you tomorrow," then neglect to make the call. In fact, to speak in the future tense, as we do so casually and offhandedly, is always a lie. It seems so trivial, but we don't regard the ramifications and we do have cosmic accountability for our errors. We must balance the ledger by correcting those errors.

The Bible provides an example of the havoc that bearing false witness can wreak: When Sarah hears the rumor that her only child, Isaac, has been sacrificed, she dies on the spot, overcome by shock.

Deception exists everywhere. To be duped can produce great harm. In the interactive system that is a human relationship, we may choose to ignore signs that a deception is being perpetrated and thereby pave the way for our own suffering. The liar and the lied-to often share equal responsibility for the outcome. The one who bears false witness must pay a price, and the one who believes the lie suffers an injury.

Almost everything we hear, almost every conversation in which we participate, is an untruth or a lie. (An untruth is a false statement that is not told purposefully, while a lie is one that is told purposefully.) Listen more closely to what you and others say, and hear the falsehoods spilling out. You'll notice most conversations are concerned with the future, the past, or a third party who is not present.

But the future doesn't exist, except as potential, and it is therefore an illusion. The past has already happened and is dead and gone. Since it no longer exists, like yesterday's news, it too is an illusion. Speaking about a third party is invariably in the nature of rumor or gossip and serves no redeemable end.

The Tenth Commandment

The Tenth Commandment says, "Do not covet." Coveting is characterized by avarice, greed, envy, jealousy, competitiveness, or possessiveness. The Tenth is an especially important commandment for modern life, particularly for how we view our life circumstances.

Dr. Faustus is a character from medieval legend who made a pact with the Devil in which he would receive everything he wanted in return for selling his soul. Today, Faust is the oversatisfied person whose every whim or desire is satisfied. The Faustian vision seems to have been borne out, almost two hundred years after Goethe wrote his famous play *Faust*, in our affluent Western society.

As we strive for ever more and insatiable satisfaction, however, we have left behind great physical hunger, illiteracy, disease, and mortality rates[3] and a general feeling of despair. In social terms, this despair results from wanting to own objects, often at the expense of others—to keep for oneself and not to share with others. We are educated to be Faustian men and women.

Coveting also connotes enslaving, removing the freedom of others. The tendency to seek ownership is expressed in the strangest places, as when patients sit across from me and speak of "*my* cancer," "*my* illness," and "*my* anxiety." They own the ailment, just as they own an article of clothing: "I have on *my* shirt, *my* pants, I'm carrying *my* book, and *my* cold is wiping *me* out; they belong to me. I own them." Or, using the word *have:* "I *have* a cold, I *have* a bank account, and I *have* arthritis." We own whatever isn't nailed down.

You must cease owning at whatever cost. Coveting involves a desire to take, keep, advance, and hold on to at the expense of others, in service of personal greatness. At the base of the covetous impulse is the fundamental error to seek to be God.

To heal, we need to own what we have created. Once done, we can then cease to own it: We dispose of it and end all our attachments to it. We can also reverse coveting on a personal and social level. Coveting is probably the most significant cause of social disturbances in America: violence, drug addiction, alcoholism, social inequality, and poverty. We can start to remedy these social ills by ending this impulse in our individual lives.

We are inculcated with the belief that it is important to be important, and hence we desire to be important—a desire that actually covers a strong feeling of inferiority. We believe that accumulating a lot of material goods makes us special. We identify with the objects we possess so that our entire sense of self-worth gets tied up in them. We tie our value to the quantity of goods we have accumulated.

The reverse of coveting is sharing, the desire to give without a desire to get. It requires a trust that we will not be deprived of what we need if we let go of what we own. In fact, without the desire to get, we are given to by the universe. It never fails!

*   *   *

In this example from my practice, a number of the Ten Commandments come into play.

Beverly was a young woman suffering from regional ileitis. She was attuned to spirit and well aware of the meaningfulness of the precepts in life, and as such she connected her ailment with being "bottled up" and "boxed in." She said that she had not revealed herself openly to anyone. When the ileitis first manifested itself at fifteen, she kept quiet about it, and no one outside her immediate family knew of her condition. She was always one to keep quiet and speak in a soft voice.

Beverly looked more deeply into the reasons she did not express herself and found out that she and her two older siblings felt that her parents had to be protected from hurt. That is, whenever anything painful happened to one of the children, their immediate response was to keep it from the parents to protect them from that unpleasantness. For example, Beverly once fell off her bicycle and suffered a nasty bump to her forehead, with a good deal of pain and swelling. She did not tell her parents about it to "protect" them. Beverly realized that when she stifled her strongly felt emotions to protect others, she experienced a "tightness" in her mid-abdomen region.

I pointed out to Beverly that by concealing from her parents the truth of her personal suffering, she was not keeping to the commandment against bearing false witness. Not telling the truth brought on feelings and sensations of tightness and finding herself "boxed in." Telling the truth would have observed the commandment of honoring father and mother and shown respect for her parents. Creating a false picture for them was, in effect, creating a "graven image," in words rather than by hands. Moreover, she had been acting contrary to the

Eighth Commandment, against stealing: She had been stealing valuable information from her parents that might permit them to confront what they needed to confront about life, that is, it isn't all peaches and cream.

Beverly realized that she did not need to chastise herself for her habitual behavior, but that she now needed to correct that behavior and become more watchful and willful in acting in accordance with the commandments. Initially, she would need to examine her actions as an objective observer, stop her impulse to protect, and say to herself that she was acting hurtfully to herself when she was.

For her imagery work, I asked Beverly to see herself as strong and then to imagine herself confined in a box that someone was shaking. She was to find her way out. She did so, pushing the ends of the container away from each other, and made her way out of the box. When I asked her what she saw, felt, and sensed, she said she felt free and sensed an expressiveness of her body, including her abdominal area. She said that she saw herself next to a living infinity sign. I asked her to see the infinity sign as the small intestine and to enter it, sensing its smooth and open flow, knowing that this was how her intestinal tract was now working. She entered and felt an immediate sense of unity with Oneness and a great transcendent joy. I asked her to keep that for herself, leave the infinity sign when she was ready, and open her eyes.

When she returned, she felt immensely free and blissful. To heal her intestinal tract, she continued doing this imagery for up to three minutes at a time, three times a day, six days out of every seven, for three weeks. By the end of this time, her symptoms had abated significantly and her digestion was becoming normal.

The Three Vows

By living the Ten Commandments, we turn toward a life of spirit and away from the constraints of illness, suffering, misery, and self-torture. To carry out the precepts, we must follow three requirements or vows, without which we cannot really make the turn to spirit. These three vows, which underlie all spiritual systems, East and West, are obedience, chastity, and poverty.

Obedience is the willingness to obey the invisible reality. When we are obedient, we attribute more importance to the invisible reality than to the princes of this world. As Adam and Eve were asked to obey the one voice, so are we. We are asked to trust the invisible and to be faithful to the One. Obedience is the practice of silencing our personal desires and emotions in the face of our conscience.

The One comes through to us as our inner voice, speaking through us all the time. In the chapters that follow, I provide a number of techniques for making direct contact with the One and listening to Its messages.

Chastity is faithfulness to the One. It means that we are not fickle and do not chase after whatever tempts us at any moment. The chastity vow underlies the commandments against adultery, coveting, and putting any god before God. Chastity involves the taming of our sexual impulse; sexuality is a direct test of chastity. To be chaste is to live without coveting, making the heart, the seat of love, the center of our activity. Chastity is the practice of love.

Poverty means giving up the need to acquire material wealth in favor of the wealth of spirit that can come from the invisible reality. Poverty does not mean being homeless or living in a hovel, or even in any sort of impoverished state. It does mean recognizing that our occupations are only a means to growth of spirit and are not the end point of our lives. The vow of poverty underlies the commandments against stealing, coveting, making graven images, and taking God's name in vain. We silence our inner acquisitiveness to receive revelations from the invisible reality.

Unless we take these three vows, we cannot possibly turn toward attunement to spirit. Taking them helps us greatly in our personal healing, as well as that of our entire race and the planet. We are entering critical times where our racial and planetary existence is threatened. It is by no means a foregone conclusion that we will succeed in saving ourselves or the planet. To start reversing the immense destruction that has already been done, it is our responsibility to take these three vows. Moreover, we must say them in the present tense, *not* in the future tense.

The Gospel of Matthew says that we ask and we will be answered, seek and we shall find, knock and the door will be opened to us. When we take these vows, we are engaging in all three activities. The truth of them will be known to us only when we experiment in the ways I have recommended. When we don't live these commandments and vows—by far the hardest tasks we face in this life—we are left with certain consequences, which we explore in Chapter 6. But we first want to look at the keys to healing and the healing relationship, which facilitates recognition of these truths.

4

The Seven Keys
to Healing

Cure people's ills, and you make them healthy
for a day. Teach them to stay well, and you make
them healthy for their lifetimes.
                                    —ancient Chinese saying

I have often been asked how techniques of will and
imagination can exert physical healing effects. One immediate explanation is that a reciprocal interaction is
constantly going on between mind and body. They are
having an effect on each other all the time. Healing the
bodymind system is a coming into wholeness and becoming healthy, and it cannot be accomplished without
the participation of mind.

Healing is both an objective and subjective phenomenon. Objectively, we can witness it happening in our

own body or in someone else's. Subjectively, we all experience healing on a moral, social, emotional plane, in ways unique to each of us. In the spiritual traditions, teachers can verify the genuineness of healing experiences.

For healing to take place on the physical and emotional levels, spiritual medicine offers seven keys to healing. These seven keys are the preparatory steps to receiving gifts from the invisible realm.

Healing is an active participatory process for those who are ill. We don't sit idly by and passively let a doctor or a medication do the work for us. The healing process requires that we contribute to our own wellness. We have to bring ourselves out of the imbalances of illness to a place of balance where we act in proportion, in a measured way, keeping a regular rhythm and a steady pace. Healing is a partnership between the visible and invisible worlds, between ourselves and God. We must take the first step, and then God responds. We must remember God, for God to remember us. This remembrance is an obligation on our part, a way of choosing life. God's promise to us is that if we choose life, we shall never be deserted by God.

These seven keys are: 1) cleansing; 2) faith; 3) forgiveness; 4) pain; 5) quieting; 6) reversing; and 7) sacrifice. All are aspects of the moral context.

Cleansing

Cleansing may be the most essential element in all healing. In healing we have to make space for the entrance of the invisible reality into and through our being. To make space for the influx of light entails cleansing away the clutter, guilt, shame, and residues of the past.

All medical practice has traditionally made cleansing a prime factor in its therapeutics. Cleansing helps restore the inner and outer environment to a state of balance. Being in a state of imbalance is tantamount to living in a state of uncleanliness.

Religious life emphasizes cleansing away our "sins." A sin is an error, a missing of the mark. Our mistakes can always be washed away through atonement. To be clean is to be sane, or sanitary.

In mind medicine the act of cleansing is mental. Mental imagery, will, and memory can correct the mistakes we have made. All the techniques in this book are acts of cleansing, geared to helping you correct your errors.

In our life experience, we attract some people to us and repel others away from us. We are capable of drawing both good and evil to us, on the physical, emotional, and social levels. These attractions influence us, sometimes beneficially, sometimes destructively. We have to take steps to remove any destructive influences from our being. When we are clean, fresh, and new, growth can begin.

I recommend that you do an imagery cleansing every morning before you start your daily activity. On a physical level, we cleanse routinely each morning by taking a shower or bath. Before that, upon awakening, do a mental cleansing. Here is the general morning cleansing that I find most effective:

Name: **The Garden of Eden**
Intention: To prepare yourself for everyday life
Frequency: Daily, in the early morning, for up
   to 3 minutes

Close your eyes. Breathe out three times. Imagine yourself leaving your home and going out into the street (descending a staircase if you normally do). Leave the street, and see yourself descending into a valley, meadow, or garden. Go to the center of it. Find there either a golden feather duster, a whisk broom, or a hand rake (depending on your preference or the degree of cleansing you need). With this tool, quickly clean yourself thoroughly from top to bottom, including your extremities. See how you look and feel, knowing that you have cleaned away all the dead cells from the outside of your body and all the gloom and confusion from the inside.

Put down the tool, and hear coming from your right the sound of a flowing stream or brook. Go there, and kneel by its edge. Take the fresh-flowing, crystal-clear, cool water in your cupped hands and splash it over your face, knowing that you are washing away all the impurities from the outside of your body. Then take the fresh-flowing, crystal-clear, cool water in your cupped hands and drink it very slowly, knowing that you are washing away all the impurities from the inside of your body. Feel and sense yourself refreshed, tingling, energized, and more awake.

Get up from the stream, and find a tree, at the edge of the meadow. Sit under the tree that has branches hanging down with green leaves. With your back against the trunk, take in the pure oxygen that the leaves emit, together with oxygen in the form of a blue-golden light, a mixture of golden sun and blue sky, that comes between the leaves. Breathe out carbon dioxide in the form of gray smoke, which the leaves take up and convert into oxygen. The oxygen is given off by the leaves and comes through the trunk, entering your body through your pores. Make a cycle of breathing with the tree, and breathe as one with the tree. Let your fingers and toes curl into the earth like roots and draw up its energy. Stay there for a long moment, taking in what you need. Then get up from the tree, and see how you look and feel.

Keep the image and feelings for yourself as you leave the garden and return to your street. Go back to your home by the way you came, and return to your chair. Then breathe out and open your eyes.

Faith

The second key to healing is faith. Faith means living in the moment and practicing to live in the moment. All healing happens in no time, as the work of the instant, the present without reference to past or future. It is not a time-bound phenomenon because it is an act of coming into wholeness, health, and holiness in the presence of the present. The etymological root of the word *heal* also gives rise to the words *health, whole,* and *holy.* We can practice momentary life. All of the exercises and techniques in this book permit this practice of faith. At the same time, we are trusting the moment and the *uncertainty* that characterizes living in the presence of the present. My teacher Madame Muscat defines *the life of spirit* as "leaping into uncertainty."

Our culture pushes us to believe in certainty as well as its near relatives, safety and security. In my own profession, it is difficult for physicians to live with uncertainty and ambiguity. But to heal, we want to work in uncertainty as much as possible. We are not concerned with the outcome or result—itself an element of certainty. Certainty is another connection to the future, one that we have been told puts our doubts to rest. But living in the future actually fosters doubts, while living in the present erases doubts.

As I shall elaborate in Chapter 6, when we practice the exercises to reverse doubt, expectation, and denial, we are practicing faith. Listening to our first voice and following it without regard for the consequences is an act and practice of faith.

It is often said that either we are born with faith, or we are not. That is not so: Faith *can* be learned. It often takes an experience such as physical illness or emotional suffering to make us want to learn this "new" way for ourselves. When the event of suffering provokes us to develop a process essential to healing, wholeness, and self-transformation, it provides a blessing.

Forgiveness

Forgiveness is the third key to healing. For any healing, we start by forgiving ourselves. We stop blaming ourselves for the errors we make. We stop judging and criticizing, and we end all self-condemnation, self-deprecation, and self-flagellation. Each of these forms of blaming is based on self-authored standards of right and wrong, good and bad, important and inferior—standards that are man-made, with no inherent validity or truth. We need to disentangle ourselves from them.

Forgiveness provides an excellent way to disentangle ourselves. As soon as we become aware of our habitual self-criticism, we remind ourselves to admit the error and ask ourselves for forgiveness. Say no to the blame, and tell yourself that you are making up a story, using your own name. Thus: "Jerry is making up a story." If the error has offended or created trouble for someone else, then confess that error to the wounded party and ask for forgiveness.

Admitting our errors and mistakes, truly embracing them, and then being loving to ourselves rather than harsh and severe evolves a wonderful healing attitude. Severity and harshness toward ourselves plays right into the hands of the serpent. We set up an idol of self-perfection, then abuse ourselves and others when we do not attain the ideal.

When we forgive ourselves, we feel lightness in our being. This lightness confirms the healing nature of forgiveness. In truth, we can't forgive—we can only *ask* for forgiveness. The response of forgiveness comes from the invisible reality.

In ancient times confession and forgiveness were intimately related. In the first century the Hellenistic philosopher Philo elucidated the method of confessing errors to gain forgiveness, and the Catholic Church later adopted some elements of this technique.

Forgive, and our burdens lighten, while our yoke becomes easier to bear.

Pain

Pain is the fourth key to healing. We are usually in some sort of physical or mental pain. In fact, we become so accustomed to everyday pain that when we are promised relief from pain by making some change, we often reject the choice. The unknown often seems much more painful than present pain. So we choose to remain with the current pain.

In such situations what we are not aware of is that the pain we are avoiding involves growth. There is no growth without pain. There are two sorts of pain: habitual pain and growth pain. Growth pain is connected directly with change and the unknown. Healing usually involves growth pain. So feared at first, this pain often turns out to be of much less intensity and severity than the original pain.

We know that pain is part of the healing process because our mental life stays up, even as the symptoms we originally experienced recur. We seem to get worse before we get better. When your symptoms recur, pay attention to your emotional and mental life. If you are feeling alert, not down or depressed, this is a sign of healing. The rules of thumb are to always choose the pain that you habitually avoid and take on the pain of the unknown. For the time being, regard all pain as your own creation. Don't treat it as "bad," but acknowledge it as having value, just as you would regard any pleasurable state as valuable. Always move toward whatever disturbs you. See it as an image, and meet it directly. Retreating from it only strengthens it.

Pleasure and pain have equal value, are equally genuine and real in the moment of experiencing. We are not well served by applying a standard of good or bad to them. Accept pain at first. Do not treat it—initially— as an enemy. You may eventually need pain-killers to dull it, but you will have been changed by the experience if your attitude toward pain has adjusted.

Quieting

Quieting is the fifth key to healing. To bring healing to ourselves through an inner process, we must be inwardly quiet. Inner quiet wins over half the battle against illness, including cancer and AIDS. A friend of mine went through a quadruple coronary bypass surgery several years ago. He was "frightened to death" beforehand and did exercises to calm his anxiety. After the successful operation he remarked that the inner work had helped him to be calm and tolerate the operation.

Once we are quiet inwardly, we can focus our inner forces on healing. Without quiet, we virtually lose the battle even before we have begun. Without quiet, we cannot concentrate sufficiently to engage in inner work. In many cases of chronic and catastrophic diseases that I have worked with, inner disquiet has had a parallel disruption on the physical level, adversely affecting immune, hormone, and muscular function. It is difficult to be quiet in the throes of pain or a spreading cancer, and in instances where it is just too difficult, medication may help to bring about a state of quiet, which then allows concentration on the inner work. The simplest way to achieve inner quieting is through breathing, specifically by alternating long exhalations through the mouth at first followed by normal inhalations through the nose. Another exercise is to close your eyes and see yourself on an elevator at the fifteenth floor. Take the elevator down to the first floor, and as you pass each floor, see the number light up. At the first floor, the doors open and you leave the elevator. Open your eyes.

Reversing

As a key to healing, reversing means making a turn in life, away from habitual attitudes and toward new possibilities. The act of remembering our relationship to the commandments is a way of reversing.

The reversing process can bring significant beneficial shifts in people's being. The model of mind medicine and the techniques of will, imagination, and memory associated with it are intended to reverse how we look at our habitual world. When we experience reversing, we naturally experience a moment of inner hope, an inner light. This hope is not a false hope like those we often feed ourselves and that others feed us. False hopes always concern themselves with the future and are always framed in the future.

Instead of thinking of the past or future, reversing allows us to return to the present and relieve the tension in our bodies. When we think of the past or future, we are in two places at the same time but not in synchrony. Since thoughts and emotions have physiological counterparts, we experience the stretch physiologically and eventually physical problems emerge.

Reversing is recommended at all times. It means that we try to change our habitual activity every day by doing or thinking the opposite of our tendency. An excellent far-reaching example, in that it is the single most important exercise for spiritual transformation and transmutation that I know of, is "Nighttime Reversing." It can also be used for depression, a malady that almost everyone has experienced in one form or another.

Name: **Nighttime Reversing**

While you are lying in bed with your eyes closed, see yourself go over your day in reverse order, event by event. Start with the last event of the day and relive it in imagery. Then go to the next-to-last and relive it. Continue in reverse order until you reach the time when you woke up. Recall each event slowly and carefully, trying to correct your attitude and behavior in those situations where you had difficulty. Also, try to obtain something that you wanted for yourself that day but couldn't get. If you had a troubling conversation with someone, recall the conversation as close to verbatim as possible, but imagine the other person's words coming out in your voice and your words coming out in his or her voice. In doing so you will understand what the other person was experiencing (if you wish you might call that person the next day to make amends). Continue this reversing process until you are able to go back to that previous morning when you woke up.

By reversing from the night back to the early morning, when we have awakened, we have moved from the dark to the light. In doing so we reverse the progression of the day from light to dark. By reversing from dark to light, we also give an instruction to ourselves to reverse depression, a movement in the mind from light to dark. Bringing light into the dark is a classical way of understanding the healing impact of mental imagery. It has always been known that the bringing of inner light—and imagination is inner light—arouses our being. So, when the dark moods overtake us, it is necessary to bring in light. The more "serious" and chronic the disorder, the more darkness is in our being.

Sacrifice

Sacrifice, the seventh key to healing, entails being able to give of oneself without regard for the result. It is the opposite of coveting. It is a payment we make that permits us to receive a blessing from the abundant invisible reality. It seems to be part of cosmic law that we pay in some manner, shape, or form, so that we may receive. So much of healing depends on preparing ourselves to receive. When it comes to healing, we cannot take the attitude of "first give me, then I'll pay." First pay, then receive is how it actually works. No one is exempt from this scheme.

The biblical story of Abraham and Isaac story exemplifies the requirement for sacrifice in a bold, vivid, and what may appear to be an extreme way. Abraham, his faith tested, was willing to sacrifice his son Isaac to obey the will of God. His story exemplifies willingness to sacrifice what was precious and loved in the material world to achieve something of significant value from the world of spirit.

Time after time, both in my clinical practice and in my everyday life, I have seen sacrifice followed by healing or achieving some benefit. Sacrifice may be understood as "letting go" or "giving something up." Don't be afraid to do so—it is a fact of our life here on earth that we give something, then get something in return. But don't give something up with the idea of getting something else in return.

Giving up something that you like or love is a kind of sacrifice. As a practice I would recommend that you give up one thing that you love each day for forty days. Give a donation to a poor person or to the charity box at your house of worship. Do not expect anything in return, and try to give anonymously. Another caution:

Do not sacrifice yourself on the altar of another person's needs or interests—it is idolatry to do so. Do not enslave yourself or give your life away. This is a sacrifice of self that is not conducive to staying well.

These seven keys to healing are the most critical and essential elements in mind medicine. If we assimilate them, where can this new model of medicine take us? The answer lies in the next chapter.

5

The Healing Relationship

...For I *am* the LORD that healeth thee.

Exodus 15:26

Perhaps the most significant contribution that spiritual or mind medicine has to make is in the healing relationship—the special relationship between the sufferer and the shepherd who is guiding the sufferer to health. Spiritual medicine reframes our understanding of the healing relationship, the most intimate, loving, understanding, and educative relationship in the healing arts. It acts as a catalyst for healing. The spiritual physician lends him or herself to the sufferer temporarily, then returns unchanged. He or she is a healing instrument, sharing their knowledge and wisdom so that the sufferer can heal.

A model of the spiritual physician can be found in an old Arabian story about a sheikh who dies and leaves his three sons seventeen camels. He has stipulated that the oldest son should get half the camels, the second son a third, the youngest son one ninth. The three sons are in a quandary, as they cannot possibly fulfill their father's wish with seventeen camels. They finally go to a sage in their community for help. He listens to their story, ponders it for a moment, then tells them that he will lend them his camel to help them solve their dilemma. He asks that they return the camel if and when they have no further need for it. They go home with the camel, and now they have eighteen. The eldest son takes his half, or nine camels; the second son takes his third, or six camels; and the youngest takes his one ninth, or two. Nine plus six plus two equals seventeen. They then return the eighteenth camel to the sage.

The story beautifully illustrates the healer's role. The sons were in some distress, experiencing problems for which they could find no ready solution. The sage did not investigate their past or make any interpretations. He did not presume to become an authority and dictate to them an answer that he regarded as the only true one. He made no judgments about them, nor offered any unnecessary prognosis. He simply *lent a hand*. In so doing he became a catalyst.

A catalyst is an element that, when added to a process, helps to speed that process forward but itself remains unchanged. A vitamin is an example of a catalyst on the biochemical level: It helps speed up biochemical processes while remaining unchanged. In our story the sage lent a hand and helped the three sons resolve their dilemma. He stood outside their situation yet became completely caring about their situation. *He had no vested interest in the outcome* and was prepared in fact to lose a material possession—his camel—if that was what it took to solve their problem. He lent a hand without vested interest, with an attitude of full acceptance of them without judgment. He himself remained unchanged, including his personal circumstances as he retrieved his camel. He lost nothing, and the three sons gained everything. This is the essence and hallmark of a true healer.

Reframing the healing relationship changes the role of the sufferer as well. I do not regard the people who come to me as patients. They are not different in kind from me. Like me, they are on a journey through this life, through an undiscovered country. The sufferer is an explorer. I am a guide for him or her, but I am also an explorer, a searcher whose journey continues even as I write these words. Likewise, my guide, Madame Muscat, led me through nine years of active exploration and always remains my beacon.

As a healer, I treasure the suffering of the spiritual seeker. I know what modern medicine does not: that suffering is a step toward healing. Physicians constantly mistake suffering for an enemy to be eradicated rather than seeing it as a necessary element in the healing process. Symptoms, including pain, may reflect a healing process rather than a pathological reaction that has to be attacked and stopped. What doctors call "symptoms" are really natural adaptational responses[1] as we try to cleanse our systems of imbalances, foreign bodies, and accumulated garbage. Cleansing responses are part of the body's healing response and must not be suppressed. Yet physicians attack "symptoms" with myriad drugs, often adding more toxins to the system, resulting in reactions many times worse than what was being treated. At the same time the medications may significantly cut off healing by suppressing cleansing activity.

By contrast, I encourage the healing response and

the *necessary* suffering that comes with the purging and cleaning out of poisons. This pain is a *growing pain* that must be not only met but lived through to enhance personal evolution. Spiritual evolution requires that as a community we experience growing pains as we come of age and that we relinquish our desires and needs for immediate gratification.

That lack of understanding about the healing process has led to a great schism between modern physicians, conventional psychiatrists and psychotherapists, and their patients. Patients have felt abused and been treated harshly, without compassion or love, and as a consequence, malpractice and negligence lawsuits against practitioners have proliferated especially over the last twenty-five years. The prevalence of these lawsuits is not simply a result of technical incompetence on the part of clinicians but is related as well to the gulf between clinician and patient.

Modern medicine does not accommodate an active participation by the patient in the therapeutic process. In fact, some doctors would prefer that patients not be active, that they not ask too many questions, and that they definitely not challenge the doctor's authority. Modern medicine is based on the authority of the doctor and the submissiveness of the patient. It is a relationship based on power and paternalism. Doctors simply do not know how to talk to patients, because of their failure to understand and accept the suffering of their patients. Life spans were never as long as now, and long-term suffering is a new phenomenon in medicine. Conventional medicine was founded on a model of acute care: helping patients overcome acute symptoms stemming from bacterial infections. Patients would either die quickly or return to health quickly. In the practice of acute medicine, rapid recovery gave doctors a misguided impression of themselves as special and godlike, possessing special powers and a great omniscience, having the answers to the great mysteries of life and death, health and disease. This godlike mask has crumbled in the face of chronic illness, long-term suffering, and the crush of new illnesses with which physicians' knowledge just cannot contend. But a spiritual understanding of health and disease can help restore communication between healer and patient.

In spiritual medicine, the healer understands that the suffering of the seeker is a result of his or her mistaken actions, beliefs, and knowledge. Each of us has created our predicament and can therefore change that predicament. What stops us is that we lack the requisite knowledge, tools, and perspective on life to make the change. Furthermore, we do not recognize the messages that our suffering tries to convey to us. Nor has anyone given us permission to accept our suffering or to explore new avenues and directions in our lives, free of judgment, criticism, and condemnation.

With a sincere attitude, the healer provides the most singular relationship that the sufferer has ever had. The spiritual relationship provides a solid foundation for healing. In spiritual medicine, with this atmosphere, explorers have singular healing results. This relationship is by far the single most important element in healing.

The healing relationship between clinician and patient can also apply to how we treat ourselves. The "spiritual friend" relationship is called the sixth relationship, the one that mirrors the loving relationship between God and ourselves. The other five relationships—parent-child, teacher-student, lover-lover, friend-friend, pastor-flock—are habitual ones, predicated on the will to power, or derived from a need that one party needs the other to fulfill. Conditions are attached to these relation-

ships: "I'll give this to you, *if you will . . .*" In mutual
need, each seeks out the other to satisfy a self-interested
or self-serving end.

The spiritual friend seeks out no one and attaches
no strings to his friendship. He does not use the other
as an object to fulfill a need; nor does he have conditions
to be met. It is an unconditional friendship, fueled by
love rather than power, with no need for an outcome or
result. It cannot be considered a "transference" relationship in the usual psychological sense, since nothing is
being transferred from some past relationship onto the
current one. It is, in fact, a relationship sui generis, without precedent, unparalleled in this world. The sufferer
has never had a relationship of this sort. The healing
relationship allows us to stay in the present for our own
sake, honors our freedom, and gives us permission to
make choices of our own free will. I experienced such a
relationship with Madame Muscat, and many searchers
experience it with me.

In conventional medicine, healing that takes place
outside the direct effects of medication is referred to as
the "placebo effect." *Placebo* means "to please," and it is
indeed the pleasing relationship—a welcoming one between the two parties—that creates a channel for the life
force to flow. Placebo also means the invisible elements
of mind, faith, and love brought into the therapeutic situation that creates the healing possibilities. Since modern medicine can't account for, or accommodate the
invisible, "placebo" is a quirk of nature. For us it is the
essential ingredient for healing; how healing can take
place without it is a miracle. In an atmosphere of real
acceptance and welcoming, the sufferer begins to say yes
to life, the invaluable first step on the road to health.
Most current medical models cannot conceive that the
personal relationship between doctor and patient could

play a significant role in healing. But this truth won't disappear. It would be foolish to listen to supposed authorities and discount the benefits of love, compassion, and caring in healing.

As a spiritual friend, I do three things in the healing relationship. First, I share my knowledge. I am not a helper; helping presupposes that one is in a superior position of authority, looking down at someone less fortunate. It is a subtle arrogance. I am sharing, not helping. What I am sharing, besides considerable knowledge, are techniques for healing. I bring techniques into the light of day and provide appropriate instruction about their use.

My second function is to enter with the explorer into the search for truth. I know for certain that no one ever gets tired of hearing the truth, and that illness represents our deviation from the truth, presented in biological or emotional form. It is a display of the accumulated falsehoods we bear.

My third function as a spiritual friend is to provide love in a nonjudgmental, caring relationship. The love I speak of here is unconditional. In ancient times the Greeks called it *agape* (pronounced "ah-GAH-pay"). It is the only true kind of love that we know. Many experiences are called love that are not. The erotic relationship is mistakenly called love, as in "let's make love," and there are parental love and brotherly love. But these forms of love always have strings attached—you generally have to perform something to get it. When you put yourself in somebody else's shoes to know how he or she feels, however, and give to that person what he or she needs without desiring something in return, without judgment, then this relationship is unconditional, with no strings. This is *agape*.

In a relationship of *agape* the healer preserves the

freedom of the explorer. She must not be concerned with results. A doctor who has a vested interest in obtaining results cannot help but want the patient to provide results. The patient then becomes an object of the doctor's need, often with dire consequences, including many unnecessary and painful tests and procedures and more and more drugs that have dangerous effects.

The spiritual friend does not try to find personal satisfaction, reputation, and economic gain at the expense of the sufferer. Doctors and healers are to avoid inflicting further suffering. Explorers and patients are to avoid adding to their own burden and refuse further suffering. The Hippocratic Oath says that the physician should "first do no harm." Healers can follow that injunction if we stop needing results. Neither doctor nor patient really needs results. Neither really has to focus on the future. Let us stay in the present.

Not only do we not need results, but healers of whatever persuasion must recognize that sufferers are free either to be ill or to be well. Illness and wellness are choices that each of us is free to exercise. This choice is akin to choosing life or choosing death. Loving the patient involves supporting him or her in that choice, without prejudice. Having embraced the healing attitude of love, compassion, and caring, I don't interfere with the sufferer's freedom to be ill. I have no vested interest in the outcome. I do not take credit for whatever gains he or she makes in healing, and I have no preconceived idea about what is normal or abnormal. I don't set a standard that the explorer must achieve. Choosing to be ill has ethical implications that affect the larger group. In the short run the suffering experienced among the larger group will continue whichever way the sufferer chooses. In the long run, it is to everyone's benefit to maintain the freedom of that one individual.[2] Cherishing that freedom, even to be ill, provides a healing environment that affects not only the sufferer but those around him or her as well.

Madame Muscat once told me that *all* therapy has a "touch of evil." What she meant was that to the extent that clinicians impose themselves on the sufferer's freedom of choice, judgment, or will, we are robbing that person of autonomy and intruding to become that person's authority. Not to be one's own authority is to surrender life. I am not speaking here of those souls whose sensorium or intellective judgment is impaired, like unconscious people or the severely mentally retarded. We serve them.

Truth is ours to seek. Love is ours to become. The ten precepts—the commandments—are ours to accept.

Truth, morality, and love are the component parts that the spiritual friend, the healer, the mind medicine practitioner brings to the relationship. The healer is in the service of God, but the healing takes place between the explorer and God.

Many people attribute all sorts of great powers to healers. The populace now idolizes healers, just as the same populace previously idolized doctors, because of a universal tendency to surrender power to outside authority, now garbed in a "spiritual" mantle.

I never met a healer—or doctor—who didn't have human problems like yours and mine. They can only be catalysts whose influence speeds up the process of healing. Once that process is started, the explorer has the responsibility to continue that process, if he or she so wishes. Many people take the attitude that healers perform magic and the sufferers simply receive it—end of story. To walk away with that story, though, would be self-delusion. The encounter is only the first step. Next you start to go to work on yourself. Not to do so is to take on the same role as the patient who does not participate in his or her own healing.

My dear friend Mary Elizabeth Avicenna is a fine healer. In one of our many conversations, she mentioned that healing generally seems temporary, that it doesn't hold over time, and that symptoms return or other symptoms show up. I ventured that the fundamental issue in healing is the value system of the person being healed. Someone else may start the healing ball rolling, but you—the potentially healed—have the responsibility to maintain on your own the practice that the healer has initiated. The healer creates a harmonic vibration in your force field, which helps bring about some order. If you don't sustain that order, then you will fall back into your old ways. To keep yourself from returning to your habits, you need to establish and maintain a spiritual friend relationship with yourself, especially as you relate to your illnesses. If you maintain this relationship and spiritual order, healing *can* be permanent.

In mind medicine, we can become spiritual friends to ourselves by assuming a new attitude toward our afflictions. We undergo a change of heart. Instead of being adversarial toward our illness, we seek to create cooperation between the illness and ourselves. We treat it as an authentic and genuine part of our being, not as an alien to be shunned and despised. Rather, it is a messenger that reflects our own inner imbalances and needs to be integrated back into our lives. The integration takes place through love. We treat the illness with love or a loving attitude. We bear in mind the ancient biblical injunction: "Love your neighbor as yourself." The illness is our closest neighbor, closer than any family members or friends. When we are in pain, we are closer to that pain than to anything or anyone else. So—love it! Again, biblical wisdom says, "Do not do unto others as you would not have them do unto you." Do not hate your ailment. It will hate you back. Replace hate with love.

Ken, a middle-aged businessman, was diagnosed with stage four malignant melanoma. He had a huge mass in his abdomen, with enormous fluid swelling. By conventional medical standards, he was "terminally" ill.

Our work, which we did by telephone since he lived in a distant city, at first consisted of mental imagery. He would see the tumor and then do whatever was necessary to correct that image. He saw a derelict black ship in the ocean floating aimlessly. He corrected the image by slicing up the ship into small sections with a laser beam, "dicing it up," as he termed it, and then seeing the ship become a shiny luxury liner. He felt appreciably better afterward, and more relaxed. When I asked him how he viewed his illness, he said he saw it as adversary, an enemy that had to be defeated. I asked him to consider switching his attitude and instead to *love* his cancer. Some people find it difficult to embrace this attitude and would rather fight the cancer like a prize fighter, and for them, this can be a commendable attitude.

At first, Ken was jolted by this idea, but since he trusted me, he was willing to try it. He did genuinely open up to loving the cancer. I explained that loving cancer is tantamount to loving his neighbor as himself, since the cancer was, in truth, his closest neighbor—a fact to which anyone who is ill will attest. He realized that he wouldn't want to do to this neighbor what he wouldn't want the neighbor to do to him. Here is what transpired over the next few days:

Day 1:
   He saw himself outside the Garden in the euphoric world on the other side of Grace. He knew that he

needed to get into the Garden to become integrated. He ate the apple, seeing the cancer as the apple.

Day 2:
He saw the image of the cancer as a nutritious dinner. He ate it with pleasure and felt well and whole.

Day 3:
He held the cancer as a toy plastic ball in his hand. When he asked for help in loving it, a magnificent goddesslike woman appeared. The ball was transformed into the house where he had lived as a child. It held no nourishment for him physically or emotionally. (He began to sob.) He became a baby in this house. The woman cradled him in her arms (more crying) and told him to sleep and that when he woke up, he would be healed. (He was uncontrollably crying now.)

Ken could not speak at this point, nor continue the exercise. He explained, with long pauses throughout and immense emotional eruptions, that he was healed, that she had placed her hand on his heart. Finally he was unable to continue. Then he said to me: "God bless you. I could not have done this without your direction and guidance." "God bless you," I replied. "So, you are healed?" "Yes," he said emphatically. We decided that that was enough for now and that we would speak again soon.

Shortly afterward, I called Ken to find out how he was doing. He said that he had experienced great changes in himself and was now calmer and more accepting of his situation. Several months later, I called him again for a follow-up. His phone number had been changed. When I called the new number, an answering machine picked up and a woman's voice gave instructions for leaving the message. I did so, although she did not mention Ken in the message. She returned the call shortly thereafter and told me she was Ken's estranged wife and that Ken had died a couple of weeks before. She said that he had called her to minister to him in his last days, which she did. He had died quite peacefully, and doing the imagery work (which she did with him during those final days) had helped him find emotional and spiritual healing that prepared him to accept death. In the imagery a woman who was glowing and angelic in appearance was waiting for him. This heavenly mother told him not to be afraid of what he would shortly face. He became quite calm then and knew that the end was near, and he faced it with great equanimity, finding repose and comfort in the angel who had come to escort him. He saw that this dying was a healing time for him, and he recognized that although death was approaching, parts of his life were coming together. He told this insight to his wife just before his passing, which was peaceful and without pain.

I think that Ken's story speaks to a most important way to view death. He had learned something new about dying and approached death unafraid. The mental imagery that he used made all the difference, as his wife attested. In effect, he had had a change of heart about himself, and he learned something significant about the illness that claimed his life. Through his change of heart he was able to receive love from an angelic presence who prepared the way for his departure from this earth.

To find love in this life is a momentous event—often in the most unusual circumstances. By Ken's own account, he found healing happening in his heart. He could not turn back the clock—it was too late for that. But he did find a new dimension of joy that carried him through dying to death.

A student of mine who works with cancer patients,

Frances Greenfield, summed up this healing attitude nicely when she said, "When the cancer comes, it assumes the overwhelmingly central place in one's life, everything else paling into insignificance. In learning about oneself, the cancer is substantially reduced in importance while the learning of the essence of one's life takes its proper place and significance. We don't deny its physical presence, and in our work we give it due attention. But it becomes absorbed into the larger picture of our life process and what we are here to learn on earth." This is the essential attitude that can start us on the road to healing, a process of integration of ourselves in physical, emotional, mental, social, moral, and spiritual terms. It is not that we deny the illness, but we see it from a different perspective. This shift substantially reduces the anxiety we feel about being ill.

In addition, healing can and does happen even when our physical symptoms remain. Take, for example, these two clinical illustrations. I met a woman with ovarian cancer when we appeared on a TV show together. She had this disease for eleven years. Her health program consisted of a number of inputs, she said, including mental imagery, dietary change, exercise, and meditation. The host asked her about the cancer itself and its status. She said that every year she went to the doctor, who checked her physical status. Every year he found cancer tumors in her abdomen, but they appeared to be the status quo over time and were not particularly affecting her life; nor was there any evidence of their spreading elsewhere. Indeed, she was living a full and active life, full of meaning and purpose, she said, which included taking care of her family.

She went on to describe a most significant point. She was healed in her life on the levels of spirit and emotion, she said. Consequently she maintained that she was healed, although the physical signs remained. The tumors might never disappear, she said, but that in no way negated the healing that had transpired. She was clear that the presence or absence of physical symptoms was not the definitive marker as to whether a healing has taken place.

She was absolutely correct, in my estimation. This idea has been echoed on a number of occasions in my own clinical practice. A woman named Julia has had breast cancer for thirteen years, but she does not use conventional treatment. She has resorted to her own will and to doing mental imagery to accomplish her healing. She lives an active, full, creative life, in fine spirits. When she experiences an emotionally critical situation, the tumor in her chest wall grows. When the situation subsides, the tumor shrinks. She says that she has been healed on the spiritual and moral levels, having made striking changes in her value system. She knew that she would not die of this disease and that it would not spread. Focusing too much on the physical level sets us up to be locked into the outcome. It makes us worry about how things will turn out, as if healing were predicated on the outcome of the physical experience. With long-standing cancer, my impression is that for some people this disease loses its virulence after a certain point and does not pose the danger that it did early on.

In the Bible, Job was the subject of a bet between God and Satan. Satan insisted that Job, the most righteous man of the kingdom, the man of greatest faith, could be turned against God. To accomplish this, everything was taken from Job: his wife, daughter, land, goods, cattle, money—and health. Job never wavered in his faith. Having passed all the tests, Job had everything restored to him, and he reached a new inner transformation. He healed spiritually—*but* his health was never restored. He remained with boils until the end of his days. The boils show us that healing is never completed, that we always have to polish the diamond of our true being. For Job, as for those with long-standing disease who have healed, the remaining physical symptoms are a constant reminder to be in the present, to be grateful to God and value our connection to Him, to be glad we are alive, and to attend to our own healing and being in the world as a task that is always with us.[3]

Healing has to do with the integration of an entire being. The integration may leave a physical or emotional mark that acts as a reminder of where we have come from. To remember prevents us from becoming smug, complacent, or inflated. Even when we become whole again, the matter is not finished. We have to continue polishing the diamond of our being. We can always slip back, and for some a mark that persists can serve as a helpful reminder to continue the work of healing.

Having set the context for wellness and illness in these first five chapters, we can now look at the specific processes that create our disintegration and subsequent integration.

6

Why We Become Ill

For as one thinketh in his heart, so *is* he.

—Proverbs 23:7

What causes illness? Why should we become sick and die? Many nonhuman creatures, after all, live to incredibly old ages. The parrot and turtle live for hundreds of years free of disease. Trees can live thousands. Yet we shrivel up and die in less than fourscore years, a mere speck in time in the context of the universe.

In this chapter I shall approach physical and emotional disintegration in human beings by looking at where it originates—in the mind. Three tendencies of mind lead directly to illness. They may all operate together, or one or another of them may be most clearly present. These three tendencies are doubt, expectation, and denial. I refer to them with the acronym DED (pronounced "dead") because they directly contribute to our demise. They are the basic constituents of physical and emotional disintegration. Our education has encouraged these mind tendencies.

In mind medicine, truth is quite simple. Essentially, it is through the three tendencies of mind that we complicate matters for ourselves. They impel us to make up stories about our life situation. Accepting these stories as true invariably leads us into an impasse.

Doubt

Doubt first asserted itself in Eden, where Adam and Eve lived an idyllic existence with no disease and no death—only everlasting happiness and eternal life. God granted them everything, while cautioning them against seeking knowledge of the physical world. He told them to listen to His voice and His voice alone. Suddenly, a second voice spoke to Eve in the guise of the serpent. He tempted her by promising her the knowledge and power of God if she ate the apple from the Tree of Knowledge of Good and Evil. So Eve found herself in a quandary, listening to two voices. Two voices—the essence of doubt. Doubt means being torn by two, as Eve was torn by two voices. She resolved her dilemma by taking action rather than reflecting and allowing her faith in the One voice to solve the situation. She did not draw back to the One voice (belief) but instead succumbed to the voice of the serpent (experience). She gave in to doubt, and she and Adam were evicted from Eden. Doubt, according to the Western spiritual tradition, is the seed cause of all emotional and physical illness in the world.

What is the source of doubt? The incredible promise offered to Eve was that she could *usurp* the role of God.

It is the impulse to usurp that underlies the experience of doubt. It is part of the will to power. Often when we are in doubt, we are afraid that we will lose something valuable or have to give it up, or we are trying to figure out what another person wants so that we can please him or her and thereby get a reward. We then let that person exert power over us—just by the mere fact of our anxiety. Doubt causes us to lose our power.

Indeed, doubt forces us to compromise in many situations. It clouds our judgment so that when the pressure becomes too great, like Eve we take recourse in experience. To satisfy the anxiety generated by the doubt, we may even resort to addiction. Inevitably, such behavior brings little reward, for it rarely if ever brings us the happiness we seek. Instead, the endless disappointments bring us suffering, misery, and pain, reflected not only in loss of confidence and self-esteem but physical symptoms. Every disappointment is reflected by a reaction in the immune and hormonal systems—in fact, in *all* the physiology of the body—which eventually causes cell and organ breakdown as our disappointment becomes chronic. The chronic nature of disappointment spawned by doubt takes us out of the stream of life and puts us on the path toward death. We are desperate to find happiness on this earth. We have to search for it, and we have to decide where to look for it. We keep making the same mistake, looking for it in the future, never believing that what we have right now is enough. We assess "right now" in terms of the quantity of goods we possess, which invariably isn't enough.

Doubt, the second voice, *always* lies. The misinformation it feeds us eventually leads us into a dead end or up a blind alley. Then we have to expend an enormous amount of energy to correct the misstep. This effort saps our will and depletes our vital human resources. With this depletion comes illness and further decay.

Here is an example of how doubt operates. Vicki was an unmarried, vivacious young woman who suffered from a severe disturbance in her eating pattern. She would binge on large quantities of sweets and other foods before going to bed. She would then awaken in the early morning, often before sunrise, to gulp down another enormous quantity of food. Vicki was not really overweight and had a beautiful figure. But she did not maintain her weight by vomiting. Rather, she kept her weight down by physical exercise.

When Vicki was invited to a Christmas party one year, she did not want to go as she did not care for the people throwing the party. But a second voice entered, saying she *should* go (in the future conditional tense and therefore automatically untrue) because she *might* (another future conditional word) meet somebody new. She knew that most of the people coming to the party were not of her social class or background. She struggled with the decision for two weeks, and she became increasingly worried about fitting into a dress she recently had bought as she was constantly struggling with her perpetual binge eating. She experienced tremendous inner turmoil and turbulence and felt herself in a state of inner emergency.

Vicki experienced physiological correlates of her inner turmoil. Worry is an emotional response that is *always* concerned about the future; although its experience is real, its context is not true. As her body mobilized itself in the "fight-or-flight" reaction to this "emergency," she suffered from symptoms of hypoglycemia (lowered blood sugar). When she experienced hypoglycemia symptoms—most painfully late at night, with enormous pangs of hunger—she would set off to an all-night deli for sugary junk food to ease the abdominal pain, sweating, jitteriness, and sleeplessness. In addition, she suffered eruptions of acne.

Everything she experienced was a natural consequence of the original doubt. The entrance of the second voice left her emotionally and actionally paralyzed, and her struggle with the second voice forced her to use up a tremendous amount of energy. On this occasion, she lost. She had been faced with a decision that had to be made instantly without looking back and without regret. Instead, she lived in indecision, which is tantamount to lying to life, and thus used up her vital resources in this unnecessary battle.

In many ways this story is not unfamiliar to most of us, although our doubts may not manifest themselves in quite the same manner as Vicki's did. Hers is a universally shared experience, although we each live it out in our own way.

Being influenced by our second voice—doubt—is a variant of bearing false witness. The Ninth Commandment says we are not to bear false witness. This could mean saying something that is untrue, or not saying something true that needs to be said. It could mean speaking a truth that need not be said at that moment. It could mean saying an untruth that need not be said. It could mean committing untruths or omitting truths. We must become aware of the many possible ways to bear false witness. Certainly the second voice speaks untruths, but it has done so ever since the serpent whispered into Eve's ear millennia ago. To bear false witness, like making an error against any of the commandments, is to choose the path of death. This choice inescapably diminishes our life force.

What makes it so difficult to resist doubt? The second voice plays on a tendency in us to want to have, acquire, and retain all that we can. The contrary tendency, which embodies the vow of poverty—to let go, give up, or otherwise divest ourselves of things, be they material objects or desires created by the mind—is not so strong. Vicki was preoccupied with finding a husband. She was worried (that famous feeling about the illusory future again) that she would not find one, and what man would want her anyway, she thought, with this eating problem. She projected herself into the future, two weeks thence, at a party where she *might* meet the man of her dreams. She was stuck between her immediate first-voice thought—"This isn't for me"—and her second-voice thought: "What could be there for me?" Through our work, she became aware of what was going on, followed the first voice, and did not go. She felt a concomitant disappearance of anxiety.

Fundamentally, Vicki's dilemma was exactly Eve's. By looking into the future to see what might be there for her, Vicki committed the moral error of usurping the knowledge and power of God. We all tend to do this so spontaneously and habitually that we take it for granted. It is supposed to be normal and is institutionalized into our educational system. But it is an untruth. As long as we continue in this error, we shall suffer the same consequences that befell Adam and Eve.

Every decision we face in our lives is at base a moral test. Life challenges us to decide whether to attempt to usurp the knowledge and power of God. The stakes are of the highest order—the cosmic Super Bowl, if you will, a matter of life and death. It is an absolute tragedy that we are not taught this truth from childhood. No one is to blame that we are not, least of all our parents, who long ago succumbed to the serpent and became shrouded from the truth.

Choose God and live. Choose the serpent and die. To live is to give up wanting to be God. To die is to beguile ourselves with the dazzling possibility of becoming God. Somewhere we need to gain the strength to withstand the serpent's voice.

Clinicians perpetuate doubt in ways that can be very subtle, especially in the area of cancer treatment. A doctor tells a patient that even though the cancer has been surgically removed, one cell may still be left in the body that could implant and create cancer again. The doctor is making it impossible for the patient ever to heal, planting a seed of doubt that leaves the patient anxious and that can germinate into a recurrence of cancer.

The physician's position of doubt is genuine, although I don't personally agree with it. Physicians invoke chance and doubt to cajole patients into accepting therapies using highly toxic and destructive chemicals that destroy a patient's immune system or even his or her body and will to live. When patients suggest that they might like to try another form of therapy, one that may be neither invasive nor inherently destructive, suddenly the doctors' doubtful attitude gives way to an emphatic certainty that such treatment possibilities are quackery. No treatment that is unproven by the standards of conventional medicine could be included in the medical model and therefore is rejected out of hand. As an example, the Canadian medical association brought legal action against Gaston Naessens, a researcher who claimed to have found a natural remedy to heal cancer and AIDS. Thousands who had been cured testified on Naessens's behalf, and the case was thrown out of court. The medical association was fined a hefty sum, and Naessens's material was made legal in Canada.[1]

For doctors challenged by patients seeking alternative treatment methods, the uncertainty of the prognosis gives way to certainty about what works and what doesn't (as if chemotherapy did work). It is convenient for physicians to be able to exercise the options of doubt and certainty when it suits their aims. They doubt that patients will ever be healed, but they have no doubt that their treatment is the only one that works. How can this approach not be suspect?

Your job as a sufferer or explorer is to carry out the Second Commandment and become your own authority, *no matter what the circumstances*. Health care providers can only offer information. They are at the service of those who seek their services and are not to dictate what decisions those whom they serve must make.

Fortunately, the voices of truth cannot be stilled. Each and every one of us is born with the voice of truth within us. We do, however, have to train ourselves to listen to that voice, to give ourselves permission to hear that voice. Generally, we do not gain permission unless we have the benefit of meeting someone who sees truth and gives us permission. When this truth was passed to me by Madame Muscat, I tried it out and found it to be true.

Physical and emotional suffering is merely a signal, a starting point for our investigation into the truth of our lives that may well lead us on a journey far more significant than a trip to Mars or another galaxy. The journey starts when we tell ourselves that we created our suffering and then ask ourselves what moral error we have committed. We recognize immediately that doubt, expectation, and denial—either alone or in combination—have inserted themselves into our lives.

I do not mean to trivialize illness. I seek to give it a balanced perspective. When we choose the path of doubt, only one outcome awaits us—death. If we choose this path, we must encounter evidence of the dying process—which is to say, disease. We spend so much energy fighting illness rather than understanding its message. We treat it as an end in itself rather than as a means to something beyond it. Its appearance presents us with an opportunity to search for meaning in our lives. It can also be a signal that our present life is coming to an end.

We need to muster our forces and learn about the purpose and meaning of illness. In doing so, we are not neglecting the illness. We are simply approaching our treatment of it from a new perspective. We do not even deny the use of biological compounds when they are indicated. They have their place in mind medicine.

I think people have to stop lending themselves to medical experimentation, which often makes their lives into living hells by creating severe discomfort, tiring them out, sapping their will to live, and bringing about effects more adverse than the illness itself.

Olga Worrall, a Methodist minister, was also a well-known hands-on healer. At one point her hands were photographed using a process called Kirlian photography, which revealed an aura of light around her fingers. Skeptics claimed that the aura was simply the effect of sweat on her hands and fingers, thrown off when ions— sodium and chloride—connected with the sweat. Mrs. Worrall went on television to debunk the skeptics' claims. A vat of nitric acid was brought out onstage, into which she immersed her hands. After a few seconds, she withdrew them totally unscathed, without burns or disintegration of skin. This in itself was amazing, but then her hands were photographed again. In the photograph the same aura surrounded her fingers. If sweat had caused the aura, the nitric acid would have absorbed it. Such healing power may exist in each of us. When we met her, my ex-wife went up to her and asked if she would heal her headache. Mrs. Worrall looked at her straight on and said, "Take two aspirin, dearie." Reportedly, Jesus suggested to his followers and people who petitioned him for healing that they take herbs and other medicaments for minor problems. He reserved his healing work for those who suffered from major problems.

Expectation

Expectation is the second element of illness. Expectation draws our attention to the realm of the future, a focus that lies at the heart of all our ills. Let me sum up how illness works. Then we can transpose this understanding to social issues.

In the Garden of Eden, the serpent promised Eve and Adam many future rewards for accepting his invitation. This promise is the prototypical deceptive act, one that is repeated endlessly here on earth. *We are all miseducated into believing that future rewards will bring us the happiness we are looking for.* From childhood we are programmed to fall for the same deception that confronted the Edenic couple. For the rest of our lives we are either caught up in this deception or trying to extricate ourselves from it, but until our eyes are opened, there is no incentive to want to break free of the serpent's coils.

Let's look at the case of Nancy in this regard. Nancy was a young woman who spent a great deal of her life trying to satisfy her mother. Although she had been married and enjoyed a successful career, she remained in emotional bondage to her mother, always expecting that if she fulfilled her mother's demands, her mother would feel satisfied and reward Nancy by acknowledging her

efforts and accepting her as a loving daughter. By seeking to please her mother, however, Nancy suffered many
consequences, including hypertension. She continually
shortchanged herself, even disregarding her own safety
and well-being, in order to please her mother. The reward she expected was never forthcoming. Each unful-
filled expectation gave rise to disappointment, to
feelings of hurt and rejection. She would then alternate
between blaming herself for expecting appreciation in
the first place, and blaming her mother for not giving
her what she needed. Her explosive anger toward her
mother had to be held in check and locked into her body,
resulting in high blood pressure. In so doing—"I'll just
keep my anger under wraps. If she knows I'm angry at
her, she'll never like me"—she effectively perpetuated
the cycle that manifested physically as high blood pressure. Learning about the insidious effects of expectations
allowed Nancy to gain control over her emotions and
her physiology, and the blood pressure returned to normal.

As we have seen, the main false belief is that the
purpose of living is to attain a nondisturbed state, to
gain pleasure and avoid pain. The serpent used a very
clever ploy here. God had promised Adam and Eve that
by listening to His voice, a nondisturbed state would
prevail, free of pain. The difference between God's
promise and the serpent's promise was that with the
serpent, the site of this fulfillment was in the future,
while God offered fulfillment in the present. In the present is where the future unfolds directly. God was telling
us that anything that happens in the present, be it pleasure or pain, is true and valuable, that our Eden is found
through the road of pleasure *and* pain. The serpent had
said not to accept pain as true and valuable and to fix
our gaze on attaining pleasure. God went on to say that

we created our own pain by turning away from His voice and not following His prescription for achieving the Edenic state. It is therefore our responsibility to face pain and use it to aid in our healing.

Like Adam and Eve, we too are subject to expectations based on promises made to us by others or by ourselves. Creating an expectation means setting up an anticipation, ideal, or standard about some future outcome. Expectation is the mental tendency to project an image of how something will, would, or should turn out. It is essentially the tendency of our minds to formulate pictures about the future. The mistake made over and over again is that the future can be treated as a truth and reality that can be planned for and even controlled. The fact is that *only* the present moment of our immediate experience and perception is real and true. The future is nothing but potential, waiting to be realized by each of us. Since it is not a factual reality, any attention we pay it is of no value and all our commentaries about it are untrue. We are not purposely telling falsehoods when we speak of the future, but the natural consequence of doing so perpetuates this falsehood and invariably leaves us holding the bag emotionally and physically.

Since expectations point toward the future, an illusory quality is built into them. We are bound to suffer disappointment when expectations go unmet, as they must. In response to our disappointment and hurt, we lash out at someone or something to blame. Often we blame ourselves and, consequently, experience anxiety, guilt, fear, anger, or any of their many derivatives, like worry, hostility, fury, despondency, envy, and jealousy. Within one to seventy-two hours of an emotional experience, we experience a physical symptom and/or an addictive craving.[2]

Although I have spelled out these steps consecutively, they all actually happen rather simultaneously and quickly, except for the lag in experiencing the physical or addictive symptoms.

It is clear that clinicians work in an area downstream from the source of illness. Yes, physical ailments are genuine and real, and it has been felt to be legitimate to catalog the names of thousands of diseases. Nevertheless, the name of a disease serves primarily to strike terror into sufferers' hearts, frightening them so that their will is depleted. Naming a disease provides essentially no information about what creates it but seems only to limit our appreciation of the contributing factors.

Additionally, by naming a disease, the clinician is saying, "Whew, that isn't me, and I am glad. My patient, whom I have just named, is now different from me in kind. I now can place him under my objective microscope and view him from a distance. Placing him in a category that I'm not in allays my own terrible anxiety about disease and death. Although I have steeled myself against death, seeing it happen almost every day, underneath I am scared to death of death. One of the ways I manage my anxiety is by gaining authority and power over my patients. Labeling them grants me authority about matters of life and death and lets me believe that I am in control." The truth is that clinicians are at the periphery of the mystery of life and death, far from the source of illness and disease. Without knowledge of DED, we can never penetrate to the heart of that mystery.

Another aspect of expectation and anticipation is *standards*. Standards are ideals, or fixed goals and outcomes. They are made either by God or by humans. All man-made standards are located in the future. They are always associated with expectations and are, of course, unattainable. They are ways for one person or group to maintain power and authority over others and institutionalize that power. Six major institutions have created these illusory standards: organized churches, the military, governments, medical arts, big business, and science. Organized churches use the standards of good or bad, right or wrong; the military and governments use standards of in step or out of step, in-group or out-group, conformists or the enemy; the healing professions, of normal or abnormal; big business, of pretty or ugly; science, of real or unreal.

Any two contrasting values that we are asked to weigh and fulfill constitute a human standard. To serve false human standards, we align our belief systems with four basic dual urges: 1) to get to the nondisturbed state by gaining pleasure and avoiding pain; 2) to gain approval and avoid disapproval; 3) to gain acceptance and avoid rejection; 4) to be important and avoid feeling inferior. Satisfying these four basic dual urges always involves the sacrifice of our own integrity or morality. For example, in order to be important a man may force others to bow to him—often by violence or murder or both—to acknowledge that importance. In addition, obeying human standards usually, if not always, involves fulfillment at the expense of someone else's welfare or integrity.

Success and failure is another human standard. Our achievements are assessed by someone else or some group, and our worth is measured thereby. Anxiety, worry, fear, and allied feelings accompany us as we "try to measure up" to this standard. When we "make it" (if we really ever do), then we become part of the "in-group" and feel assured that we will remain in the precincts of power.

Where false standards and the will to power exist, love does not exist. Love reflects our willingness and ability to put ourselves in the shoes of another person, to give to another without expecting or demanding something in return. Love does not seek self-aggrandizement or self-inflation. Nor does it look to dominate others or impose conditions before a connection can exist.

Denial

The third element in the destructive DED triad is denial. Denial is the mind's tendency to avoid acknowledging a reality or truth. We deny the characteristics in ourselves that we find to be distasteful or undesirable, or that don't conform to our self-image. Denial, in short, is the refusal to accept our wholeness or inherent unity, which includes all our potentials, even those we erroneously label "bad."

Whether it is an inner perception, or a thought, feeling, or sensation, or something external to us that we find distasteful, we turn away from it, or sweep it under the rug. The key point here is that whatever we turn away from will continue to make its presence felt, bringing on endless disturbance and disease. Until we pay attention and acknowledge our denied issues, their disturbing presence will never leave us. What we deny consistently arises, and what we resist persists. We enter physical and emotional turmoil as we try to push away the disturbing issues. Eventually, that which we deny clouds our lives, forcing us to push it away, wearing us down until we succumb in disease, aging, and death.

As a tendency of mind, denial has a connection with mirroring. When an interaction we have with someone

disturbs us, we are *always* seeing in the other person a
denied characteristic of ourselves that is being mirrored
back to us in that person's behavior. Take, for example,
Janice, who chronically complained about the selfishness
of her husband. Exploring a little further, I found that
she was distressed that others had also behaved selfishly
toward her over the years. She quickly realized that selfishness was her own denied quality. To Janice, I suggested that this quality had been with her throughout
her life. Since she did not embrace or even acknowledge
it as a genuine and authentic tendency of her own, I
explained, it would follow her unrelentingly until she
addressed it. She reflected on the myriad times and
events when selfishness had determined her relationships and dictated her behavior. I proposed that she be
"selfish"—whatever the definition of *selfish* was for
her—for twenty-one days, without regard for the consequences (the future). Doing this, Janice admitted, in an
unprejudiced and unbiased way, a genuine and authentic quality back into her existence. When we permit our
denied characteristics to appear—when we are willing
to undertake this work—our life circumstances change
in profound and welcome ways. What amazed Janice at
the end of this cycle was how attentive her husband had
become toward her.

The disturbing quality we deny has a holographic
nature. The denied characteristic in fact has roots far
back in our personal past and is a core belief around
which we organize our lives, reflecting the entirety of
our life experience. A single instance reflects the whole
of our life. Denial of selfishness had been Janice's way
of relating to the world—*from girlhood to the present*. She
used considerable energy and resources to hide that
quality from the world, to avoid manifesting selfishness
toward anyone. The consequence was that selfish people

entered her life, took advantage of her "unselfish" nature, and left her feeling chronically irritated, angry, and mentally and physically depleted. Her life force was being slowly eroded away.

Another clinical example of the workings of denial is the case of Wilma. Wilma suffered from migraine headaches for twelve years. She tried every conceivable treatment known to conventional and natural medicine. She had originally become aware of headaches during a recovery program that helped her overcome her alcohol addiction. She had done a good deal of thinking about the "source" of the headaches, which often lasted up to twelve hours. She developed a "theory" that they had to do with feelings of anger.

Wilma, who worked as an addiction counselor, set extremely high standards for herself and expected perfection from herself and others—a problem many of us have. She envied her fellow counselors when they did a good job or were praised by the head of the clinic.

At the same time, she experienced difficulties in relating to her husband, Mike. Throughout her life, she had toned down her intelligence and assertiveness in order to prop up his. Mike was an able provider but was fundamentally a passive man, and when his business failed, he was unable to reestablish himself. It turned out that Wilma had really provided the impetus when he initially started his business. She did not want to recognize Mike's passivity or what she perceived as his weakness. Although she really loved him, she knew that the headaches and anger were directly related to her distressing feelings about his weakness, as well as her feelings of envy and competitiveness in the clinic. She realized that the anger and headaches were related to each other, that they were physical and mental analogies of each other.

Anger seemed to be connected to her never-ending expectation that Mike would once again be able to provide her with the comfortable life she had known. But this expectation was not being met. Although she was a woman of considerable strength and intelligence, Wilma did not utilize these qualities to direct her family. She had witnessed her own pattern in her parents' marriage: Her mother had merely stood by while Wilma's father had floundered in his life. She was living out the family error, transmitted psychogenetically from her mother.

In the application of spiritual medicine, I approached Wilma's difficulty by first giving her the tools to counteract not only the migraine pain, but the anger and envy, her tendency toward expectation, her denial of her desire to be taken care of and be passive, as well as her denial of her anger and Mike's real passivity. The educative input was to reframe her relationship with her husband, to bring it into balance and provide for further growth.

I made it clear to her that it would be to her benefit to use her strength and intelligence to bail her family out of their financial plight. Many women who grow up in male-dominated families subdue their own capacities and prop up their husbands, whom they may perceive as weak. Some women continue to follow the male judgment, even though they may suffer from his errors. I assured Wilma that Mike would be relieved if she took over and lent her strength to the family's situation, while at the same time she would correct the error that had been passed on to her through her mother's line. Asserting herself would surely have a beneficial effect on her marriage, and on her anger and headaches. She had to stop denying her abilities and start being honest and truthful. Truth is the healer—it is surely our best medicine.

Wilma had faith in the truth of what I was saying, and she faced the truth of her marriage and took on her long-denied role. The effects of her action were remarkable. Both her own and Mike's vigor was renewed. He began openly to rely on her judgment, and with Wilma's intervention, his failing business began to turn around. Her anger melted away, and her confidence grew by leaps and bounds. She blossomed as she made new discoveries about herself.

Along with this bold step, she did imagery and will exercises to alleviate the migraine headaches and her tendency to set up expectations.

We know now that DED is the mechanism for aging, decay, disease, and death. Wilma now had to watch over herself. She had to become a thought manager, observing what she thought and said and paying attention to thoughts and verbalizations that crept up on her that had to do with expectations. She had to anchor herself to the moment and not wander away from herself.

As we have seen, the experience of anger is real, but its context is not true. Wilma discovered the truth of this fact as her life turned around dramatically, both at home and at work. She became headache free for the first time in twelve years. As of this writing, it has been three years since her last one.

As long as the medical model holds that the body and mind are not one, it can *never* see the mind—not to speak of social, familial, and moral contexts—as matrices of illness. Broad economic and social repercussions will occur if spiritual medicine becomes widely accepted. The costs of my work with each person are far less than those incurred through modern medical treatment. Work attendance and productivity vastly improve with spiritual medical treatment. The need for drugs decreases, as does the number of office visits. Insurance companies in general have not yet seen the benefits of this approach, but one person avoided a costly operation that would have cost thousands of dollars. He filed an insurance claim for only a few sessions that healed the tumor. The insurance company fought him over the reimbursement, even though they had been saved an extraordinary amount of money. To them, mental imagery was not a bona fide medical treatment, and that was all that mattered.

Let's look at another example of denial. Alice had suffered from insomnia throughout her entire adult life. Very often, she had been cheated or taken advantage of by people, while she regarded herself as eminently fair and a person of impeccable integrity. But she discovered that she used to take advantage of people when she was young and had turned away from that quality by denying its existence. She never confronted its presence or took responsibility for it. Later in life, consequently, she kept being besieged by disturbing experiences until she realized that our experiences are the reflections of our beliefs in the mirror of the "external" world. The experiences that disturb us have a way of grabbing our attention. A disturbing experience tells us that we have cut ourselves off from our full humanness by failing to embrace an authentic trait in ourselves. We prejudicially keep ourselves from saying yes to an aspect of ourselves because we have deemed that aspect bad. Walt Kelly, the creator of Pogo, once said in Pogo's voice: "We have met the enemy, and he is us." Until we embrace all our qualities as authentic for us and all our beliefs as genuine, they will come back to haunt us.

Alice came to recognize that as a girl she had made a vow *never* to cheat, and she had made every effort to reject this quality. The quality thereafter "followed" her, as it were. When she became aware of this situation through our work and acknowledged openly these cheating tendencies—which she could now appreciate— the disturbing experiences stopped for good. Now that the secret belief was out in the open, was accepted and *owned*, it could now be disowned. Denial gave way to the only real control we have in life, the control over our beliefs. Any other need to control, i.e., others, the world around us, circumstances, is a disintegrating factor that ages, decays, and kills us.

The technique for reversing denial is twofold. First, you recognize immediately that what is disturbing to you reflects a denial tendency. The nature of the disturbance defines the tendency, as Alice's case shows. After she realized and embraced her tendency to deny cheating, Alice took the second step: She used mental imagery to decrease the belief that she was a cheater. She imagined herself being enveloped by the belief, as if it were a bubble or large pod, then bursting free from it and seeing it disappear. In this process she reversed the denial, rather than succumb to it, then took control of the idea, exerted an act of will to dissociate herself from it, and then passively let it disappear. As a complementary process, I suggested that she "cheat" (whatever that term meant to her), especially those who were currently cheating her, for twenty-one days, without regard for the consequences. For her, it became a matter of cheating the cheaters to make them feel what it is like to be on the receiving end. This is, indeed, a most compassionate act to those who act destructively.

For whatever the reason, denial is a prejudice against ourselves. We say no to authentic parts of our being that, once rejected, will always come back to haunt us. We *must* continue to bump into those experiences— social, interpersonal, emotional, and physical—until we acknowledge and accept all realities, unpleasant as they seem to us, as our creations. Remember, also, that those who behave destructively have the responsibility to face their actions, and have accountability for their actions.

As I stated before, we are made in the image and likeness of God. As such, according to the Western tradition, we embody the capacity of God to *create*. We are creators every one of us.

A creation can be either a temperamental disposition that we are born with, or a character trait we have inscribed into our own being. It may be any thought we experience as a belief or opinion. Creations are like our mental children who become autonomous beings and, like physically created children, have a certain energy of their own and demand attention, nurturance, and feeding. They want us to do their bidding and can exert control over us. Whether these creations will be to our benefit or detriment depends on our choice. Until we accept responsibility for all our creations, we are bound to suffer.

Putting an end to denial opens a great door to freedom. It is certainly painful to accept that we have created awful things, like cancer, in our lives. Once we get through the grief over what we have done—*which we will do* with acceptance—we will gain the understanding that we are quite powerful. If we are powerful enough to create a dire process like cancer, then we are powerful enough to decreate it or create something beneficial to ourselves by opening ourselves to the power to love ourselves.

Shirley's case illustrates the operation of doubt, expectation, and denial. A middle-aged woman, she had suffered from a chronic nagging cough and upper respiratory irritation for over two decades. She had one child, a daughter named Gina, with whom she had the most difficult relationship she had ever known. Gina's behavior in general and toward Shirley in particular was always a source of irritation. Shirley had become pregnant in her early twenties, had been highly ambivalent about the pregnancy, and had even thought at times of terminating it. It was to prop up her unrewarding marriage that she had originally decided to become pregnant, but shortly after she gave birth, she left her husband.

Early in Gina's life, Shirley realized that her daughter was intelligent, high-strung, volatile, and self-absorbed. Shirley was most disturbed by Gina's volatility, a trait she shared but denied in herself. In late adolescence, Gina became an alcoholic. Shirley spent much effort denying her dislike of her daughter. "After all, she is my child, and I have to take care of her," she said after a recent falling out, about which she complained bitterly.

Then Gina gave birth to a child. Shirley wanted to see the baby, but, still angry at her daughter, would not visit.

What actually was going on here? Shirley had had grave doubts about having this child in the first place. Doubt led right into denial and expectation, which operate here hand and glove. Shirley constantly denied her own volatility and her dislike of her daughter, as well as Gina's manipulativeness and turned away from facing it, replacing it with expectations about her daughter that Gina could not possibly fulfill. Each of Shirley's disappointments encapsulated and renewed the doubt, expectation, and denial and was reflected directly in her cough and respiratory irritation.

Doubt, expectation, and denial take an enormous toll on our existence. There is no pain without denial, for each expectation is a form of denial. Every time we create an expectation, we are denying our immediate perception of the present in favor of something to come. We deny our present circumstances for the sake of future ones. When the present is not providing us with the immediate pleasure we seek or is painful, we develop an expectation. As it has to in such specious circumstances, the expectation is not filled. Out of this situation of expectation and disappointment, we begin the process of illness, aging, decaying, and disintegration. Illness begins with the trials and tribulations of life. Healing begins when distressing situations are corrected. These corrections certainly involve the physical component of the illness, but they also include the factors that have brought on the physical or emotional disturbance. Addressing the *source* of illness leads to the illness clearing itself up. Illness is the effect of these mind tendencies. To work solely on the illness without taking the source factors into account is merely putting the proverbial finger in the dike. Working at the source level brings the mind directly into the mindbody equation. Spiritual medicine does not deny the existence either of the mind or the body or the necessity of attending to the needs of both. We address healing of the body with our mind medicine treatments, to be sure, as our approach brings the two together for a healing of the whole, not just of bodily symptoms.

Doubt, expectation, and denial support moral error. If we believe that we don't have everything we need, if we don't have perfection in this world, we strive to attain it. When we doubt, we believe that our course of action may not yield the perfection we think is obtainable in the future, and we look for a better option. When we expect, we are directly seeking perfection, a misguided human standard, that we believe we are supposed to achieve in the future. When we deny disturbing elements, we do so because they don't fit our picture of perfection. We are not perfect if we are mean, conniving, or thieving. In fact, perfection really means the *wholeness* of ourselves, "good" and "bad" qualities. Our every trait or quality is encompassed within that wholeness. So nothing is "bad" or to be excluded.

Doubt, expectation, and denial all act upon the present moment of experience to *negate* it, to make it appear that it is not good, doesn't exist, or has little of value to offer. If we are greedy for something beyond our present experience, doubt helps us make ourselves or others into objects of worship, idols.

The greatest experience any of us can ever have is that which shows us that we are not God. This realization requires relinquishing the urge to power and accepting humility, for we don't need power to achieve happiness. The paradox is that by replacing the will to power with the will to love—itself involving caring, humility, and giving—we experience the happiness and freedom we are looking for. The techniques for displacing and reversing doubt, expectation, and denial that are provided in the next chapter will help you on your way. The first significant step in this process is called "becoming a watcher."

Becoming a Watcher

There is only one essential way to *begin* coming to grips with doubt, expectation, and denial. It is to become a *watcher*, an observer or witness of these tendencies.

It is not hard to become a watcher, and it is the imperative first step we all *must* take to take charge of our minds and become a thought manager (a phrase given to me by Adrienne Samuels, an occupational therapist in the New York City area). Becoming a thought manager requires learning to experiment with ourselves and becoming attentive to the presence and activity of the three tendencies.

We practice watching for DED in us over a period of time, ranging from days to weeks to several months. As I pointed out in my book *Healing Visualizations*, it takes three weeks to change a habit. This includes physical problems as well. It may take several three-week cycles to effect change. We can experience this change directly. It does not take place by insight or by intellective understanding. There is a distinct difference between insight and change. To know does not necessarily lead to change. In fact, most times it does not. *Change begins by doing*, by taking action. From that point, knowledge comes. Watching is the first step in doing. Once we get used to watching, the practiced technique becomes an automatic and ongoing aspect of our being, ever and always.

In becoming thought managers, we become our own personal sentinels. We observe our thoughts, speech, and behavior. Step back for a moment from your direct immersion in experience to observe how you are operating. Offer a commentary on your relationship to your present reality. Look for how you are living out of the present moment and projecting yourself into the future or the past. Listen to your inner thoughts and your verbal language. Listen for the future and past tense. Once you become aware of your habitual use of them, make a note to yourself of the inner comment that you have been making up a story or have been telling yourself an untruth. This steadfast practice leaves you with a unique experience of feeling lighter, as though a burden were lifted off your shoulders. The process of telling yourself the truth, stopping yourself from reflexively accepting the barrage of falsehoods coming at you from everywhere—from "out there" and from "in here"—is unending.

Becoming a watcher and gaining an awareness of truth are intimately linked. A "still small voice" of truth speaks to us all the time, even though it is persistently drowned out by the noise and static of more blatant untruths. The axiom of spiritual medicine is that *everything worded as a vow or promise in the future tense is a lie*. The same is true for the past tense. Perhaps close to 100 percent of our conversations with others are about the past or the future. But our incessant thinking and believing about the past and the future loads us down and uses up an incredible amount of mental and physical energy as we bear up under them and remain alive. When we are weighted down, our entire being is down, including our immune and hormonal system. Our strength ebbs under these conditions and can finally give out in exhaustion.

The present moment is the place where there are no disquieting emotions. In the present is calm, peace, and a feeling of happiness. When we become light, our whole being is lifted, and our immune and hormonal systems are up as well. All happens together if we believe, as I do, in the unity of body and mind. If we are not in the present, we are living in a mirage, an illusion that perpetuates our suffering and eventually does us in.

The practice of watching is an important way to get back to the present. We want to reverse the wish of Michael J. Fox, who wanted to get back to the future (three times, no less). I want you to author a new book that paraphrases Freud's *The Future of an Illusion* and call it *The Future Is an Illusion*. Get a little pocket notebook and title it just that. Begin making notes to yourself about your self-discovery. Begin to understand that your illness is a blessing that has provided you the opportunity to start this work.

How do we recognize doubt, expectation, and denial? Doubt is experienced when we have to face a present decision. Expectations have to do with projecting thoughts into the future. Denial deals with tendencies developed in our past that we want to disown.

Doubt is easily discovered. It begins in our own inner dialogue. It always makes itself known as the second voice in our consciousness. We have the impulse to do something or make a certain decision—*but* suddenly another voice intrudes and gives a contrary impulse. We find ourselves caught between two voices in what I call the Adam and Eve Syndrome.

With this understanding, we can watch our doubts with new perceptiveness. When a doubt arises, acknowledge it, know that it is the second voice, know that a usurping impulse lurks, and remember that there is no need to take power, except over yourself. As soon as you loosen the hold on your need to exert power, the doubt begins to melt. Relinquish that second voice, which really isn't very important. As soon as you confront the doubt, you can then take the action involved with the first thought. *Always* take that action. As soon as you do, the doubt will dissipate. The watching actually has prepared you to take the prescribed action. The continuous practice of this method breaks the power of doubt.

You can become as aware of expectations as you are of doubt, again by beginning to observe how you speak to others. Watch yourself leap into the future, ceaselessly creating conclusions about how things should work out. When you become aware of such thoughts, simply make note of them and tell yourself that you are making another false expectation. Then observe how often your expectations are unmet. We take it for granted that expecting is a natural way of life, but keep track of the movement of expectation, make notes to yourself, and say: "There goes [your name], making up another false expectation." Or: "I am observing [your name] making up another false expectation." This technique, developed by Bob Gibson, is an excellent way to defuse the power of expectation. When you speak to yourself using your name, you are speaking about yourself in the third person. You are talking about yourself to yourself, and you are becoming even more observant. You take the force out of the expectation.

Denial is easily recognized by becoming aware of the difficult situations that you confront daily. Train yourself to read the glyphs of your daily experiences. Whenever you experience pain in a given circumstance, denial is at work. A good question to ask yourself when you are in a painful situation is: "What have I denied here?" The question will often generate an answer. You have to be honest and frank with yourself. Just becoming aware of the denied issue is a significant step in achieving change. Confronting the denial is salutary, because it gives you the opportunity to own whatever it is you are trying to disown. All of us have been trying to disown something; now we have the opportunity to make corrections that will bring us into harmony and balance.

The remedy for DED is to become a watcher. Becoming a watcher is a great gift to give yourself. It obviates your dependence on some outside authority who presumably knows more about you than you do. It beats spending years of time and money talking about your life in a therapist's office, talking in groups about "co-dependency" or some other buzzword, or running off to a health practitioner whenever you experience physical symptoms, often spending money needlessly. The more we talk, the more we become absorbed in our own musings and lose sight of ourselves. We cannot talk and watch ourselves at the same time. We cannot follow the explanations and suggestions of health practitioners and watch ourselves at the same time. To watch ourselves is to become an authority on ourselves.

In addition to the watching exercises, the following mental imagery exercises can be used to help reverse DED:

For doubt: Close your eyes and breathe out slowly three times. See a serpent snaking toward you. Breathe out one time, and throw a curse back at this serpent that has come to curse you. Breathe out one time and follow the movement of the serpent away from you, knowing that you have cleared out doubt. Open your eyes.

For expectation: Close your eyes and breathe out slowly one time. See your expectation as a physical form, and rid yourself of it by burying it, burning it, sinking it in water, or letting it be carried away by the wind. Know that as you do so, your expectation disappears. Open your eyes.

For denial: Close your eyes, and breathe out slowly three times. See yourself naked into a mirror or on a blank screen (like a movie or TV screen). Repair whatever defect or disturbance you see there. Then turn the mirror or screen over, and on the other side see the new you. Open your eyes.

Do these exercises each time you work on the DED tendencies.

I've used the word *explanation* in a somewhat negative light, since we have a tendency to accept explanations as being facts, and consequently we let them act as guideposts directing our life decisions. But this acceptance is one of the most inhibiting factors imaginable.

Only experimentation can tell us if a received explanation is really a fact. If we do not experiment, we will always be at the behest of some outside authority, subjugated and enslaved. Explanations, like logic, are not truth. Things may sound true and have the ring of authority, but without authentication by our own experimentation, then everything is nonsense.

Everything is nonsense. This phrase was first uttered by King Solomon nearly three thousand years ago. It means, for our purposes, that anything we experience in the framework of DED is utterly untrue.

As you accept the need to practice thought management, please make a pact with yourself not to blame, victimize, condemn, or judge yourself unkindly or beat yourself up if you forget to practice. Every judgment is essentially a lie. It is a story or opinion (a form of story) that we make up. By blaming, you hold yourself accountable to an untrue, self-imposed standard.

Watch! Listen! Correct! That is the ticket to reversing DED. Let us now turn to how we become well and examine the essential remedies for becoming well, choosing life, and perhaps overcoming death.

7

How We Become Well

What is remembered lives.
> —*Egyptian Book of the Dead*
> trans. NORMANDI ELLIS

Becoming and staying well requires that we pay constant attention (watch) to our well-being, as well as correcting our errors. Correcting *reverses* what we have created, whether it is a disturbing thought or feeling or a disturbing action. To make a correction is to *reverse* the error.

Three functions of the mind can be used to facilitate this daily attention and correction. These are: voluntary will, imagination, and memory. They go by the acronym VIM, which also means life. Their functioning permits us to become whole and to stay attuned to life. When you practice VIM in an ongoing way, you achieve and maintain healing.

In utilizing the VIM functions you are employing

techniques to reverse your habitual ways of thinking and acting. For instance, relying on your intuition through a process of mental imagery rather than on logic to solve a vexing problem may be to reverse your usual approach. When we heal ourselves by using our minds rather than by using a pill, when we use VIM to reverse DED, we create ourselves anew.

Voluntary Will

Voluntary will is a mental spark that kindles our imagination to do something, which we may then do through the use of our musculature. The spark or desiring will initiates the process of making visible what is invisible.

Will itself can be divided into two parts: the desiring will, the spark that initiates the process, and the intentional will that provides direction and constancy. Will is not the goal but our way and direction toward the goal. It involves a constancy of activity, holding to a course through focused concentration, much as a helmsman steers a ship by concentrating on the wheel. A goal is the outcome or result of this intention. The goal is the future prospect, while the intention is our present process. Two examples will suffice to clarify this most important point.

First, a gardener has an inclination or spark to grow food (desiring will). He prepares the ground in a concentrated, constant manner in order for it to receive seeds. He plants the seeds as the culmination of his intention (intentional will). The seeds then may or may not grow, they may or may not become fruit. Fruition is the goal of the planting, but that goal is actually not in the farmer's hands. The future of the seeds depends on their

relationship to outer forces such as weather, soil conditions, insects, animals, and of course, God.

The second example is that of an archer. He has an
inclination to shoot an arrow into the bull's-eye of a target (desiring will). He follows the spark by lining himself up to aim at this target (intentional will). He
positions himself by directing his body, the bow and
arrow, his arm and hand, toward the bull's-eye. At the
moment he releases the arrow, he closes his eyes (as described in the book *Zen and the Art of Archery*) so that he
is not invested in the goal or outcome of his action. The
arrow takes flight on its own, so to speak, to hit or miss
the bull's-eye. Whether it hits or misses depends on the
forces of the invisible reality with which the arrow is in
connection.

In sum, the spark or desiring will is characterized
by momentariness and initiates a process. It can be
drained away by illness, as well as by drugs, alcohol,
and certain forms of music, like heavy metal. Intentional
will is characterized by constancy and focused concentration.

Intentional will focuses our attention on a behavior,
thought, or feeling in order to rouse our *slumbering free
will* to life. We seek to heighten this attention and give
it direction, so that we can change a habitual behavior,
feeling, or thought. By our increasing awareness, we can
take steps to change the habit. Through the persistence
of voluntary will over time, old habits are broken and
new ones can be inserted. While I have already noted
that it generally takes three weeks to break a habit no
matter how long you may have had it, let us consider
physical symptoms to be habits as well. The activity of
will through attentive awareness is *meditation in action*,
or active meditation. To activate this will, we use a disturbing situation as a teacher, which reminds us to set

our voluntary will in motion to correct the situation. We are then able to derive value from the same painful situations that we have been erroneously taught to run away from and to treat as inimical.

The function of will asserts itself very early in our lives through the creation of habits. All of us are born with free will, although it is continually challenged by patterns of thought, feeling, and action that operate so automatically that free will can seem virtually absent. However, will is always there and can be trained. Bringing will under our control is an effort directed toward awakening ourselves, overcoming doubt, and stopping expectations.

A number of techniques for vanquishing DED are presented in Chapter 8, but here is one that deals with changing a characteristic or trait, so that you can see it is possible to do. First, identify the disturbing trait. Then, enact the contrasting or opposite trait by a conscious effort of will, without concern for the result. For example, Bob, a young man I worked with, complained that he continually found himself in relationships in which he was treated badly. His superior at work took his research and published it under his own name. His wife refused to clean the house or make meals, so he had to do the housework after working long and difficult days. He maintained that he had to behave decently to those individuals and to many others who treated him in the same manner. As a child, he had learned that he should act decently toward everyone, no matter how they treated him. By virtue of these "good" acts, he would reach the kingdom of heaven.

Upon closer inspection, we discovered that his behavior was predicated upon his fear of unleashing and flexing his own power lest he become corrupted by it. Some years earlier, he had been world champion in a sport that required individual skill. After attaining his championship, he noticed that wherever he went, people catered to him. When he walked into a room, people immediately rose in recognition of his "greatness." He said that on these occasions he could "taste" the power that was then his. That taste stimulated in him the urge for more, as well as the fear that he would become corrupted. In reaction, he denied his urges and fears and put on a face of pseudo-humility to protect himself. As a consequence, his resisted feelings were now mirrored back to him, as it were, in the guise of the people who wielded power over him.

My prescription to him was to act "indecently" toward everyone for twenty-one days, without regard for the result. That is, his decency was to be replaced by its opposite. He was to practice this reversal in much the same way that he practiced his sport, where the perfection of form, mechanics, and technique—in short, the process—replaced the outcome, which would take care of itself. He had to embrace the quality of indecency and regard it as authentic so as to be able to achieve balance. He had to consciously apply his will to experience *the opposite, and thereafter a balance would be struck.* At this point he could make the decision to discard the troublesome trait or not.

Remember, you cannot disown what you do not own. Persistent denial never permits you to own a quality that is a genuine part of yourself. But ownership gives you a semblance of real control in your life. It is what goes on inside that you can control, not what happens in the outside world. The practice of opposite tendency is the general principle to apply when you become aware of denial.

When Bob contacted me at the end of the twenty-one-day cycle, he reported a noticeable change in his marriage. Suddenly, meals were appearing on the table and the apartment was clean. He had broken away from his superior and was looking for new work opportunities, and he was starting independent research.

Imagination

The second antidote to DED is imagination or, in its practical applied method, mental imagery. Inner images are the inner language, the true language of the mind, of inner life. Images are the inner glyphs, the universally shared social language of the human race. Whereas verbal language creates barriers and promotes discord and separation, images bind and unify us. They reflect the experiences we all go through rather than the differentiating aspects emphasized by verbal language. The images of dreams, reveries, and fantasies are the direct way that can help us shape and create our everyday reality.

What is imagination? It is actually three things rolled into one:

1) *A level of reality.* Our physical world is not the only existent reality. Myriad invisible realities that are as valid as our physical reality can be subjectively perceived, experienced, and lived. This imaginal reality is bounded neither by linear time nor physical space. Its world of images exists between the world of sense perception here in the objective reality of everyday life, and the world of highest consciousness where there is no image. It is a realm of *no* time and *infinite* space, where all knowledge of all that was, is, and will ever be is stored. Dreams are an example of such a reality familiar to nearly everyone.

2) *An organ of perception.* This organ lies "behind"

our ordinary sensory reality—that is, behind what the five senses perceive in the physical world of physical space and linear time. This organ of perception can be trained to gain access to the vertical reality.

3) *A mental process.* This process brings our inner language into focus when we direct our will toward our inner life. Imagination is the process of inner recovery of the image language that gives us direction. Imagination is the inner light cast into the darkness of our inner space, revealing what is there. That revelatory light is experienced as *genuine hope.* Imagination is the enzyme of the mind, analogous to a physical enzyme that catalyzes a physiological process. The inner mental enzyme speeds up inner transformation by showing us the way and giving us direction.

Imagination functions as a process of self-transformation or self-transmutation. *Transformation* means a change of form that a living being (plant, animal, or human) goes through in the process of its existence. For instance, we transform from birth through successive stages of physical and emotional maturation. *Transmutation* means a change of one form into a completely different form. For example, a caterpillar transmutes into a butterfly. This process is also called "alchemical." Alchemy is the process of creating transmutation. It is commonly referred to as a work of changing lead to gold on the material level of physical life. We understand the practical application of spiritual medicine as an alchemical process of changing the lead of illness into the gold of healing. This process of inner growth and healing is twofold:

a. *It is a process of creative imagery.* Using it to deal with an everyday problem, we see the problem and quickly correct it in our imagination. It allows us to see something old in a new way. Once the new way reveals itself in a situation, we can then take a different course of action and change our way of relating to the situation. The change we effect alters the situation forever and unalterably, in a beneficial way. This activity is a creative one, a work of art on which we each place our unique, indelible stamp.

b. *It is a process of discovery, transformation, and rebirth.* Imagination allows us to explore our inner space to find the various levels of reality into which we can penetrate, and from which we can extract information. Such knowledge can be brought back to our everyday world to transform our lives. To make the inner journey is to participate in a momentary death with respect to the everyday life. Reemerging transformed is a process of rebirth. Such inner imagery work was involved in the initiatory practices of Mediterranean spirituality, as it made its way from the temples of ancient Egypt, to the Jewish schools called the Sons of the Prophets, on to the Hermetic schools of Greece and Rome, and eventually into Western Europe. Imagery work permits a spiritual turning and movement toward union with the invisible reality. This inner journey is called Waking Dream. Its first and clearest explication is to be found in the Bible in Ezekiel 1:1, where an entire waking dream experience is described. This form of imagery work needs to be done with a guide and can last anywhere from thirty minutes to two hours.[1]

Mental imagery is the form that will takes. Whereas techniques of will are formless activities, the complementary techniques of mental imagery produce three-dimensional forms or images. (Remember that we are speaking of inner realities that can't be measured or quantified.) Will, like memory and imagination, is an invisible force. Will is made visible or given form on an inner level through the function of memory (personal and collective images of the past) and imagination (images of the present and the potentials and possibilities that we may fulfill personally and collectively). The images of imagination (mental imagery) show us the direction our will may take, what we may possibly make present for ourselves in our life experience. Mental imagery reflects our possibilities in our inner mirror, where we can see, hear, smell, or otherwise sense them. Suddenly the invisible becomes visible, and we can see our direction in life. Since the mind and body work in unison, mental imagery functions as a mode of communication from the mind to the body. Through it, the mind instructs and reminds the body about coming into order. Imagery work reveals information and new options or directions.

For example, a young man named Fred was severely depressed. He felt that he had no direction and that his life was slipping away from him. His doubt and indecision were extreme, to the point of being paralyzing. He told me that he was in a large black hole. I asked him to close his eyes and see himself in this large black hole.

Fred found himself at the bottom of the hole and enclosed very tightly within it. He was scared. I asked him to have a light, to see his surroundings and to find something there to help him find his way out. He saw light coming in from the top, but it was not enough for him to see at the bottom. He brought in his own light and found that the walls were smooth and slippery, like ice. I asked him to have on shoes with spikes and to have mountain-climbing equipment, with spikes, pylons, and ropes, to hoist himself out of the hole. He did so, but the smooth walls began to quiver as he climbed. He stayed with it, though, and climbed out of the hole.

He found that it was night and he was looking up at a beautiful full moon. He felt much better and rather more joyous, although he still feared being in the dark. I asked him to see by the light of the moon and bring in another light of his own if necessary.

Now Fred saw himself in the center of a meadow, alone. I asked him to summon the inhabitants of this meadow to him. When he did so, a tribe of men appeared. They were quite friendly and took him to their leader, who was to be his guide. His name was Shaman. Shaman had the tribe bathe Fred and dress him in a white robe. Fred was then taken to the center of their circle where he was initiated, and Shaman told him that he would learn all the tribe's knowledge of the secrets of life. Fred felt awed and happy to have found such benevolent and spiritual people.

I told him this was his place, and these were his people. He was free to come here whenever he wished and that his education there would continue uninterrupted. Shaman gave him a gold disk and told him to place it in his heart. Fred did so. He thanked Shaman for his help, bade good-bye to the tribe, returned to my office, and opened his eyes. I told him that whenever he felt depressed, he was to imagine the golden disk in his heart, to trigger enlivening feelings. Fred had discovered his own antidote through imagination to his habitual feeling. I have observed this process countless times in my practice: *Finding the opposite image brings about a resolution of the disturbance.*

In the garden of the reality into which we are born and that we have to tend throughout our lives, we spend plenty of time weeding and seeding. The weeds are images based on our miseducation and self-serving desires. They have misled us, and we have to rid ourselves of them. We use mental imagery to weed them out. No two thoughts can occupy the same mental space at the same time. Corrective images pull out the weeds, and once they are gone, the ground is ready to receive seeds. These are the seeds of new possibilities, or mental images. The seeds are now free to grow because the weeds can no longer overcome them. If we plant them, tend to them, nurture them, and protect them, they will take root, and we can harvest their fruits and benefits. Imagery work is a mental seeding and weeding process.

In another example, Stan, a young man in his mid-twenties, had suffered from ulcerative colitis for over eight years. He had taken many medications during this time, including the most current treatments available. Nevertheless, his condition had worsened, so that by the time he came to see me, he was suffering with an anal fistula and arthritic changes in his knees. He was walking with a cane.

An articulate fellow, he was pursuing a career in media. He was quite gifted in many ways, and he knew that many of his peers envied him his accomplishments. He was a person of light, and like many people of light, he attracted into his orbit people who had a dark side, who are envious, jealous, and covetous. He knew that he tended also to let people take advantage of him. His own victimization, he knew, reflected his own impulse to take advantage of others. He was highly socially oriented and sought public acclaim for his accomplishments. His interest in media was motivated in part by his desire for public approval. In his work he struggled to suppress his victimizing impulses.

We began imagery work immediately, and he agreed to suspend taking his medication while he was engaged in our work, although his primary care physician continued to follow his condition. Within two weeks of beginning the imagery work, the swelling of his knees receded and the colon inflammation cleared up. He became asymptomatic, discarded his cane, and resumed body-building work that he had previously had to abandon. The mental imagery he used included finding the inflammation in his anal tract and applying blue and white laser light to it. He saw the inflammation heal and normal cells grow into the area and through the fistula tract, healing that as well. Then he brought the laser light to his knees.

To remedy the arthritic swelling, Stan used the "Tide" exercise. He saw himself on a beach, lying with the soles of his feet pointed toward the ocean. His body, except for his head, was completely covered with sand, and water lapped up on the beach. He saw the tide come in quickly, seeing, sensing, and feeling its spiral currents enter him through the soles of his feet, move through his feet, up to his ankles, into his legs, and to his knees, cleaning out all the debris and toxins, washing away the wastes, massaging the muscles, ligaments, and tendons, seeing them all elongating, and leaving them glistening white. The spiral currents massaged the cartilage of the knee and kneecap, as he was seeing them become glistening white. With the sand-and-water compound acting as pumice, he cleansed the outer surface of his knees and his hamstring muscles, clearing away all the dead cells. He then got up from the sand, dived into the ocean, and swam out to the horizon, breathing in the pure air from the horizon. He saw his legs stretching way out behind him, supple and strong, his arms far out in front of him. After he reached the horizon, he turned around and came back to the shore in a backstroke, his legs kicking way out in front of him, his arms stretching way out beyond his head, his body becoming extremely long, breathing in the pure air from the horizon. When he reached the shore, he came out of the water, let the sun dry him off, and put on a robe he found on the beach, knowing that his arthritis had cleared up. He repeated this "Tide" exercise for twenty-one days, twice a day, in the early morning and at twilight.

How mental imagery works can be understood through a scientific analogy. Cells in the body have an electrical potential, and they oscillate at various frequencies. These electrical frequencies are invisible, but they are visible to the naked eye as color. Different colors thus represent the presence of light, which lets the invisible be seen. All body cells emit light, a reflection of their oscillatory vibrations. A shift in the oscillatory frequency of the cells produces a change in the light—it becomes trapped in the cell and cannot be emitted. If the disturbed oscillatory frequency can be reregulated and the vibrational rate balanced, healthy cell functioning ensues. This is the working hypothesis for the field of vibrational or electrical medicine that is now springing up in the United States. Dr. Robert Becker, an orthopedic surgeon, has demonstrated how bone union can be accomplished by electrical stimulation of the fragmented ends. For centuries psychic healers have used the light or aura surrounding a person to see the electrical potentials of the body. The physical and emotional body emits different-colored lights that reflect that individual's physical, emotional, and intellectual state.

In my view, mental imagery work has a regulatory effect on our physical, emotional, and intellectual functioning. Imagination is the inner light of the mind and channels the light of the universal energy into our bodies. In sending the light and truth of imagination through us, we regulate the body's oscillatory frequencies and return to a state of harmony and balance. All life is movement and rhythm. The advent of disease indicates that the movement has become static and the rhythm has been altered. Imagination reestablishes the inner movement and rhythm by sending light into darkness. All light is movement and rhythm. Sending the inner light restores the body to movement and rhythm—so that it becomes alive.

When we see what is possible for us, an inner push of will impels us to make all those possibilities into lived facts. We take what is inside us and make it an outside event. We do this all the time with injurious images—anxiety, fear, worthlessness, lack of confidence, and worry. Now let us reverse this process and use images that are beneficial to us. Rather than let the disturbing images run rampant, let us bring the corrective and productive images to the forefront. In that way we create a new environment for ourselves.

Memory

The third antidote to DED in VIM is memory, the process of becoming mindful. To remember is to become aware and awakened. The importance of memory in healing has its roots in the ancient Egyptian civilization. The Hermetic spiritual wisdom that informed that culture and served as a wellspring for all of later Western culture knew very well the significance of memory. A dominant theme of that wisdom is portrayed in the mythological story of Osiris and Isis.

Osiris was the god-king of Egypt who ruled the world between the living and the dead. He weighed the souls of the recently departed to see to what worldly realms they would be sent. His wife Isis was the goddess of wisdom. Seth, Osiris' brother, was envious and wanted to wrest power from him. He murdered Osiris and cut him into fourteen pieces, burying each of the pieces in different parts of Egypt. Isis, upon hearing of the deed, set about re-collecting the pieces. After *re-collecting* him, she sought to put him together again by re-membering him, by putting the members of his body back together. In the myth Isis holds out the fourteenth piece, the penis. As a result of this lack of wholeness, man must search for his missing member. For the ancients, that member meant knowledge. Man must search for knowledge to become whole, and Isis, the goddess of wisdom representing *all* women, is the teacher. She, like Eve, has the woman's role in life: She is the teacher of man and leads him into life. She *re-membered* Osiris and by doing so restored him to life. She resurrected him.

The possibility for resurrection, as I experience it, lies in the function of remembering. Let us dissect the word *remember*. A *member* is a part of the whole, as a limb, breast, or penis is part of a human body. A member is also a person who belongs to a group. *Re* means "again." To *remember* is to become part of the whole again. The implication of remembering is that we have forgotten something. In fact, we continuously forget for almost every waking hour of every day that we are part of the whole, that we are in God.

In remembering, Isis corrected the memory of the disturbing event. She remembered Osiris anew and thereby restored him to life. She put his members back together again, physically and mentally. She said that mind and body are one. To remember is not only physically to restore a person's members but *also to recall through an act of memory* the wholeness of that person. To remember is to make whole physically and mentally through memory. Isis re-collected Osiris. That is, she physically collected the pieces and mentally collected him again, bringing him to life again, in a mindbody unity.

A comprehensive medical system must include this mindfulness. We must become mindful of our need to re-collect ourselves physically and mentally—to *remember* ourselves. Mind medicine teaches us how to re-member ourselves physically and mentally, so that we can no longer doubt or deny ourselves.

To take charge of our own healing, we have to get out of the future and the past and back to the present. In a sense, we *remember* ourselves as whole and healed, beyond past experiences or future expectation. Much of what pains us is the memory of something painful from the past. Such memories lie at the heart of what was once called "war neurosis" and is currently called "post-traumatic stress disorder." This current label gained its use at first for Vietnam veterans who had "flashbacks," in which something they experienced in the "now" threw them back to the "then."

I first observed this phenomenon when I ran a psychiatric ward at Valley Forge (Pennsylvania) Army Hospital during the Vietnam War. We were the largest receiving hospital east of the Mississippi at that time, and I saw more than a thousand returnees from Vietnam come through the ward on their way out of the army. Many of these young men suffered terribly from "flashbacks," especially when they heard news about what was happening back in Vietnam, or about the deaths of buddies, or about some unspeakable atrocity. Their "flashbacks" were intensified by the residual effects of frequent hallucinogenic drug use in Vietnam, mainly LSD.

This extreme disturbance of memory follows a classical stimulus-response reflex arc. When we have been exposed to a repeated stimulus (an experience or event), we learn to respond to it in an automatic, habitual way. The pattern becomes ingrained over time, and our response becomes quasi-biological and reflexive. In fact, embryologists have discovered that each bodily organ has a brain, which remembers the experiences that this organ has gone through. In effect, events are stored in each organ and can be recalled by that organ when a stimulus reminds it of them. The stimulus, in turn, elicits a habitual response from that organ. This stimulus-response event is known as a conditional response (not the misnomer *"conditioned* response," which is commonly used instead; the response is "conditional" upon the presence of the stimuli). Only a molecule of stimulus is needed to set off the reawakened memory. Since we are prone to repetitive behavior, we are most vulnerable to stimuli that elicit habitual responses.

We seek to interfere with this patterning and change it in mental imagery work. We do so by substituting a *new memory* to act as a buffer between the stimulus and the habitual response. *We do not change the fact of what has happened to us*, which is impossible in any case. But we can change our memories of such facts. We can change how we choose to remember a fact and our attitude toward the fact.

You can practice a simple technique for effecting this change. Remember your original, disturbing event for an instant, thereby acknowledging its truth. Then breathe out slowly with your eyes closed and *correct* your memory of that event. That is, change your memory of it, or change your attitude toward it. Then breathe out again and open your eyes. Repeat this imagery experience each time you experience the disturbing memory. This technique helps you put a buffer over your old memory. Now, whenever the stimulus comes again, it hits up against the buffer and cannot get through to the original memory anymore. Eventually, that stimulus-response arc loses its power in our lives.

This simple yet extraordinarily powerful imagery exercise is uniquely effective and brings instantaneous results. Here are some examples:

Lydia was constantly concerned about not doing things "right," about not being "pretty enough" or "intelligent enough," and so forth. I asked her to describe the image she associated with these oppressive thoughts. She said, "I'm under a rock." I asked her to experience this momentarily and then to correct the image, knowing that as she did so, these oppressive thoughts would disappear.

She described the correction as seeing herself struggling out from under the rock and standing up straight. She climbed on top of the rock and held her head up toward the sky. She commented on how free she felt and sensed a connection between her straightened posture and freedom. I told her to do this exercise each time she experienced the oppressive thoughts. She was to do the exercise for only a few seconds on each occasion, over a period of twenty-one days.

Roberta complained about compulsively feeling she had to clean herself after touching almost everything. She washed constantly, after touching anything she believed was imbued with contaminating germs. I asked her to identify the image associated with the compulsivity, to experience it momentarily, and then to correct it, knowing as she did so that the compulsive thoughts would disappear. She described a "being behind me forcing me to do something I don't want to do"—that is, forcing her to clean. She then turned around and saw herself garbed in a protective blue cloak, directly confronting this being and ordering him to depart from her. As the being cowered in front of her, she suddenly felt strong. Facing the fear made it nonthreatening. I recommended that she do this imagery work whenever she experienced the compulsive urge for twenty-one days.

Philip came to see me complaining of lifelong respiratory allergies and a horrendous relationship with his mother. Our work focused on imagery work for the allergies and on correcting his relationship to his mother. I asked him to encapsulate his relationship to his mother in a single image that would represent its entirety. He recalled that at age eight or nine he had been sitting on his bed and his mother was standing over him, berating him soundly for something she had wanted him to do that he had refused to do. This image represented his general perception of their relationship. He then closed his eyes, went back to the scene, and corrected the image, seeing himself standing up and towering over her so that she became meek and quiet. After three weeks of carrying out his imagery program, his allergies became less debilitating. At the same time, he was able to become angry at his mother and stand up to her. Consequently, he could contact his denied anger at her. The allergic symptoms abated considerably, and he felt less rancor toward his mother.

Myra suffered from multiple sclerosis. She described what had befallen her with great sorrow. Feelings of sorrow were not new to her; she had experienced them throughout her life. I asked her to describe the image of sorrow. Spontaneously, she saw a tree with all its branches bent and contorted, all covered with black shrouds. I asked her to correct this image, knowing that as she did so, the sorrowful feelings were disappearing. She saw a spontaneous image of the tree becoming straight and tall, with its branches going up to the sky. I asked her to become as the tree. She became tall, strong, and beautiful. My prescription to her was that every time she felt the sorrow, she should correct the image of the contorted tree.

In another instance, Sylvia came to see me after suffering severe traumatic experiences. She had functioned extremely well before she had these experiences. Subsequently, she had doubted herself in many ways, doubting even that she could really ever overcome the damaging effects of these traumas.

I asked her to describe the image of doubt. She saw a black hole. I asked her to correct this image, knowing that as she did so, the doubt was disappearing. She saw herself sewing up the black hole with golden thread. She experienced a sense of great relief. As usual, I educated her to correct the black hole every time she experienced doubt for three weeks.

In a number of instances in my practice, past abuse has been healed through correcting the person's memory of it. Sometimes the abuse is remembered as rape, traumatizing a woman so that her sexual life as an adult became inhibited. For her, each time the sexual act is about to take place, the sight of the penis provokes the original response to the abuse. Even in these severe instances, the traumatic effect can be reversed. It takes consistent practice to introduce the new pattern, but the results can be gratifying.

*   *   *

Every spiritual system in the world has in its discipline the common element of dehabituating or deconditioning. Deconditioning is presented in elaborate ways, as in Tibetan Buddhism, and in sparse ways, as in Zen Buddhism. Whatever the presentation, however, deconditioning is at the heart of the practice. In the Western forms, we connect to our presence in the world and use events as a spark to our will to establish a new pattern. Breaking free of old habits releases much energy, because we no longer have to attend to and function in the old way.

Take, for instance, Daniel, who in his mid-forties maintained an abiding anger at his mother. His image for their relationship was a memory from when he was six years old. He was with his mother in a department store, and he created some sort of commotion that irritated her. She grabbed Daniel by the ear and pulled him out of the store. Customers were laughing at this scene. He felt humiliated and embarrassed, and furious with her. He never forgave her for this event. I asked him to recollect that event and to correct the image by remembering it in a new way. He recollected the scene, and as his mother was dragging him out of the store, he took her hand from his ear and clasped it in his and looked up at her. She looked down to him, and they walked out of the store hand in hand, smiling at each other. Following this correction, his anger toward his mother abated. He contacted her and established a friendly relationship with her after decades of rancor. These episodes can be multiplied by the thousands in my own and my students' work. They reflect the power of memories and images in allowing people to change their lives, to correct the errors of their existence, and promote healing.

Memory is divided into four distinct types: factual, logical, moral, and vertical.

Factual memory is the one we are trained for as children. As children, we are taught an immense number of objective facts about the world. As we get older, we are trained to use *logical memory*. This memory allows us to make sense of all the facts, so that we can use them. Later on, *moral memory* allows us to provide value or meaning to our behavior. If factual memory tells us what happened in our lives, moral memory tells us how we lived. *Vertical memory* is that memory that we use to try to make sense of our behavior and place it in a covenant relationship with God. Each time we take a moral action, we have an opportunity to remember ourselves and our connection with God. When we are not living the commandments, we do not remember ourselves or our connection with God.

Factual and logical memory involve our outer relationship to the physical world. Moral and vertical memory involve our inner relationship to the invisible world. Factual and logical memory cannot substitute for moral and vertical memory, nor can moral and vertical memory be denied their place in our lives.

Conventional psychology has not precisely understood the meaning and effect of memory. Psychoanalysis and allied psychological treatments have been concerned only with factual and logical memory. The recall of the past has to do with our personal history with our parents and others significant in our lives. Psychology also concerns itself with the aberration of logical memory known as schizophrenia. This aberration is typified by a fundamental flaw in syllogistic logic: John has a red sweater; Jim has a red sweater; therefore John is Jim. This fallacy is called *identification by the predicate*. The work of Carl Jung immensely broadened this psychological view of memory. Jung placed memory in the realm of the "collective unconscious," a repository of mythological, archetypal memories (that is, memories that exist ahistorically) that have an impact on our lives. We live them out when we act out archetypal themes in our individual lives.

Here we take memory another step and on a slightly different path and put it into relation with God. Every moral act that we perform, every moral thought we think, reawakens our remembrance of God and restores our attachment to the One authority. Becoming mindful of our relationship to the commandments, seeing how each of our actions fulfills or does not fulfill the commandments, and making the correction if they do not, is a practice of remembrance in itself.

Basically, remembering starts with asserting and training the moral memory. Moral memory ultimately recalls us to two fundamental precepts: to love our neighbor as ourself, and to love God with all our heart, soul, and might. These two precepts reflect the real essence of our Being. As we decondition ourselves, we will naturally find ourselves loving the visible world (our neighbors), and the invisible world (God). Because we are at the interface between God and the world, we come to love ourselves.

What are the techniques for deconditioning that expand those described in Chapter 6? We find them as we move into the next chapter.

8

Becoming Your Own Healer

Exercises

This world of imagination is the world of Eternity.

—WILLIAM BLAKE
A Vision of the Last Judgment

Once we accept the challenge of confronting our DED tendencies with our VIM functions, we unlock the door to new possibilities for healing and become our own healers. Mind medicine brings us to a vision of healing that is quite old and has a long history in the Western tradition. It offers an extensive array of techniques for dehabituating and reversing DED.

As I have indicated, healing initially depends on

breaking habits. This chapter conveys further dehabituating techniques to provide more possibilities for healing. They are categorized as involving either will or
imagination. Like all techniques associated with mind
medicine, they all require us to provide the aim for
which they are to be used.

The techniques described throughout this book can
help you develop your intuition exquisitely. Listening to
your first voice is really listening to your natural intuitive function and is a way par excellence to develop it.
You may be divorced from this function with concomitant feelings of loss of *self*-power and belief in yourself.
Practicing the exercises in this book will remedy all that.
To facilitate the process, do not judge yourself: There
should be no self-criticism, self-condemnation, or self-
flagellation. Do not be harsh on yourself—simply do the
work! If you slip or make an error, there is no need to
comment on it. Just fix it!

Here are the types of exercises covered in this chapter:
- imagery exercises
- mirror exercises
- spiral exercises
- Life Plan exercise
- stopping exercises
- decreation exercises
- chanting
- prayer
- exercises for resurrection

Imagery Exercises

General Instructions

Mental imagery succeeds in direct proportion to how successfully you can turn your senses away from the outside world and toward your inner realm. Once you are turned inward, you can create a mental image that can stimulate your physical body. The image will come to you on its own, as long as you direct your will and attention inward.

You may find that exercises that I have designated for a specific use apply to other difficulties with which you are coping. This is perfectly acceptable, since mental imagery exercises have a "crossover" effect and can be used for different purposes.

Body Posture

The most effective body position for imaging is what I call the Pharaoh's Posture. Sit upright in a straight-backed chair that has armrests, your back straight, your arms resting comfortably on the armrests, and your hands open, palms down. Your feet should be flat on the floor. Neither your hands nor your feet should be crossed during the imagery work; nor should they come into contact with any other part of your body. This arrangement is part of keeping your sensory awareness focused away from external stimuli.

Throughout the ages, the Pharaoh's Posture was assumed by royalty who sought their inner guides before making a decision. It is a posture expressing the search for inner guidance.

A straight-backed chair is best because a straight spine permits awareness to infuse our attention. Lying

down, in either a horizontal or a reclining position, is associated with sleeping and reduces the heightened awareness required for mental imagery.

Sitting with your back straight also enhances your breathing; your lungs need this vertical posture in order to expand fully. Awareness of breath, as all ancient physicians and healers knew, promotes greater alertness and attentiveness to mental processes. We become more attuned to our inner life as we become more conscious of our breathing.

While the Pharaoh's Posture is ideally suited to imagery work, sometimes imagery must be done without it—for example, when you are experiencing anxiety. In these situations, you may do the imagery work standing up, wherever you may be.

Breathing

Breathing plays an essential role in all inner-directed experience. Those who meditate become relaxed and quiet by counting their breaths. The Chinese equate breath with the mind itself. Yoga exercise, natural childbirth, martial arts, running, or any other sport involving concentrated intention all focus on breath.

Most of us are not generally aware of our breathing. Nor are we usually comfortable directing ourselves to our inner life. We are an active people with urges to conquer the outside world and master nature. But the inner life holds the cure to our physical and emotional imbalances and promises harmony between body, mind, and spirit. Breathing allows the inward turning to occur; it is the link that enables us to discover our personal imagery.

To enhance your images, give yourself the intention of becoming quiet and relaxed. Breathe rhythmically, in through the nose and out through the mouth. The exhalations through the mouth should be longer and slower than the inhalations, which are normal and easy—neither labored nor exaggerated. Breathing out longer than breathing in stimulates the vagus nerve, the major quieting nerve in the body. Originating at the base of the brain, in the medulla, this nerve extends down through the neck and sends branches to the lungs, heart, and intestinal tract. Influenced by enhanced exhalation, the vagus plays a role in lowering blood pressure, slowing the pulse, heart rate, and muscular contractions of the intestinal tract, and reducing the respiratory rate. When these functions are quiet, your attention is more fully available for imagery work.

I stress exhalation over inhalation because breathing to quiet the body begins with an *outbreath*, not an *inbreath*. The more usual in-out breathing stimulates us by exciting our sympathetic or excitatory nervous system and the adrenal medulla, which secretes adrenaline. Out-in breathing, on the other hand, stimulates the parasympathetic nervous system and the vagus nerve, which help the body quiet down.

When you are comfortable with your breathing and feel ready to begin your imagery work, *breathe out three times*. This may sound odd, but it is quite simple. You breathe out, then in; out, then in; then out again—for a total of three outbreaths and two inbreaths. After this, you begin your imagery exercise, breathing regularly.

During your imagery work, your attention will be focused on the images, and your breathing will take care of itself. When the imagery event has ended, you may take one outbreath before opening your eyes.

It will take you only a few seconds to establish this reverse breathing pattern. Exhaling first and inhaling second will become second nature once you have learned to image.

Length of Exercise

Do each exercise quickly! The value of imagery lies in the light shock that it gives to your system, which promotes healing. You need only a spark, only the flame of one small match to set off all the fireworks. Healing is prompted by this sudden jolt. Healing through imagery is like the homeopathic process in that a minute amount of substance stimulates the body's healing response. The rule of thumb for imagery work is that *less is more*. The shorter the imagery, the greater its power.

Imagery stimulates inner movement. We experience this vital inner movement as sensation or emotion. While sensations are physical, emotions are inner mental movements analogous to physical movements, themselves acts of will. When movements occur inside, they are life. Imagery is the form that that movement takes. If you experience a stimulus or shock, from either an external or an internal source, you respond. Therefore, making your imagery move you inside will mean that it is potent.

It does not have to take long to experience a sensation. The sensations vary from person to person and problem to problem, but they often include twitching, pulsation, heat, itching, pain, tingling, a buzz, and the like. Once you have felt the sensation, the imagery has done its work. If you don't feel a sensation after a relatively short period of time, do not strive for it by repeating that particular image. Instead, try another one.

Many think that expending more effort brings more results, but with imagery the opposite is true. Most exercises in this book take up to or about one minute to do. Many people feel that this is less time than they could or should be spending, particularly for serious ailments. Their anxiety creates the idea that they must "spare no effort." But strenuous application of effort is simply not necessary in imagery work. Once you have done an initial imagery experience, you need only little reminders to stimulate your body's recollection of healing activity. You need to practice imagery, but it should not become an obsession. One trigger is all you need to promote physiological repair mechanisms. The Russian psychologist Ivan Pavlov conditioned dogs to salivate at the sound of a bell. In imagery work, we condition ourselves to stimulate healing with a mental image. Like Pavlov's bell, the image is the stimulus, and like the dog's salivation, the healing process is the response.

Imagery exercises are constructed to stimulate the sympathetic nervous system and induce the "fight or flight" response, prompting the adrenal gland to pour out adrenaline. Once the body responds, you use other imagery to bring on a quieting response that will adjust you to the waking world after opening your eyes. Here is an example of an imagery exercise:

Name: **The Double-Edged Sword**

Close your eyes and breathe out three times. See yourself holding a double-edged sword. Swing this sword from your chest to an obstacle in front of you. Then draw the sword back again and swing the sword through the obstacle, knowing that if you refuse to swing through the sword hits the obstacle and rebounds back to you, the blade edge cutting you in half (shock). Know that when you cut through the obstacle that you are becoming decisive (quieting). After finishing, breathe out and open your eyes. (This is an excellent exercise to overcome indecision.)

In sum, true imagery is short and does not require a prolonged preliminary period of relaxation. It does not state what will be discovered in advance; nor is a predetermined outcome defined. The best exercises begin by giving a shock; then comes the correction, followed by a sense of triumph. Shock, correction, triumph—these are the three elements around which you may construct your own exercises.

Time of Day
In general, I recommend that you perform imagery exercises at the beginning of the day before breakfast, at twilight, and at the end of the day before you go to bed. Each of these times is a potent transition point: between sleep and waking, day and night, and waking and sleep, respectively. In some instances, the time you perform an exercise will be determined by your specific ailment. So

for pain, you might do an exercise every five minutes, for swelling every half hour, for a cough every two or three hours.

Imaging at the beginning of the day is a particularly good time since it is good preparation for the events and activities to come. Incorporate it into your daily waking-up and washing ritual, before doing any morning activity except urination. It sets a positive attitude for the day ahead.

How we begin each day profoundly influences how we operate and relate to people for the rest of the day. Many people have noticed that waking up from an unsettling dream can have a disruptive effect on their mood and behavior. Sometimes we simply "wake up on the wrong side of the bed" and face the day grumpily, making mistakes at work, or getting into arguments. Setting a balanced mood with an imagery exercise is helpful in determining your outlook and mood for the rest of the day.

Applying Imagery

At the beginning of each imagery exercise, I give its name, its general intention, and the frequency with which it should be done and for how long. (In regard to the purpose of an exercise, remember it is *your* intention that counts!)

I often recommend that an exercise be done in cycles: twenty-one days of using the exercise, then seven days off. This cycle parallels a biological rhythm present in all of us, most visibly in women, who are used to a cycle of about three weeks of hormonal regulation followed by about a week of menstruation.

If you succeed in accomplishing your intention before the prescribed cycle is complete, you may stop the imagery if you are so inclined. But some chronic illnesses or ailments may not be healed after twenty-one days. Additional cycles of imagery practice are recommended for these more chronic ailments.

Your eyes should be closed for all the exercises, unless otherwise indicated. If closing your eyes makes you feel uncomfortable at first, keep them open. Start where you feel comfortable. (Children and young adolescents often feel more comfortable with their eyes open.)

In certain exercises, I make no reference to breathing out. This is not an oversight. For these exercises, closing your eyes is enough. After a while you will instinctively know that no special breathing is required for certain exercises in certain situations.

You may find that when you are imaging, you are witnessing yourself doing something, and you are aware of two of you. With practice, that should change so that witnessing stops and you are simply there. You are no longer doing imaging in the third person but in the first person.

Creating Your Own Imagery Exercises

You may find yourself spontaneously modifying the exercises as you go through them. Go right ahead. Let whatever comes up for you emerge. If you find your own imagery, use it. Participate in your own healing.

Cleansing
Seek to create imagery that is cleansing. Cleansing is an essential ingredient in healing. You can do it through imagery of golden brushes, water, brooms, feathers, airstreams, and so on. A spiral current of blue

water can be quite effective. Find any means of cleansing that suits you.

Imagery Sources

There are a number of significant sources from which you can derive imagery exercises. These include your conversations, the dictionary, and books of great worth to you that bear words of truth.

The dictionary is a tremendous stimulus for creating imagery. There you can find words defined, then broken down into syllables. At first, look at the definition to find an image. If that doesn't yield one, look at the etymological root word. Often root words yield images. Indeed, that is exactly what I did in devising exercises for thyroid healing. If the syllables don't yield a pictorial stimulant, then you can find one in the definition or the etymological root of the word. Investigate this root word. From it, you can derive many words, pictorial in quality, that are all organically connected. For instance, for the word *thyroid*, the root word has to do with "forest" and/or "door." An image having to do with a door or a forest can immediately suggest itself for a thyroid-healing exercise.

The *American Heritage Dictionary* is an excellent dictionary for this purpose, as it contains an Indo-European root dictionary at the back. It is an indispensable tool for making imagery exercises. Under the word *prostate*, for example, are a number of imagery-laden root words that, put together in a lyrical way, will bring forth an imagery exercise.

You may suddenly find yourself becoming a poet, creating images from your own creative source that become the tools for your own healing. After using an exercise a few times, you may shed the words, and the only instruction you need give yourself is to simply do the exercise.

Conversation is another source for imagery exercises, especially conversations where we describe our circumstances in terms of an image. If you hear yourself saying, "I feel like I am at the bottom of a well," then create an exercise where you move out of that well by climbing up. Bring with you whatever tools you need to make this climb. In imagination there are no rules.

A man named Jimmy once said to me, "I want to stop this temerity—I mean timidity." When speaking of timidity, he revealed the impulse he was blocking, which told him that he could construct an imagery exercise to "go from timidity to temerity." He could see an image that *for him* is associated with timidity, acknowledge that image for a few seconds, then see an image of temerity. He could thereby set up a new possibility because he could *see* a new way. Imagery opens the door to new possibilities.

Like a tightrope walker who can't get to the other side unless he sees himself on the other side first, Jimmy went from timidity to temerity knowing that he was becoming bold and reckless.

Reading is another very useful way to find images. For instance, in the *Encyclopedia of Things That Never Were*, I recently came across an entry for "Sparti." I discovered that for the ancient Greeks, Sparti were the fiercest of warriors, so fierce that when they had no more enemies to destroy, they turned on each other and destroyed themselves to the last man. They were employed by King Cadmus of Thebes. Using this imagery I created a cancer-healing exercise that is excellent for those predisposed toward aggressive imagery. (Not everyone likes aggressive imagery, and for them such imagery is counterproductive.) The exercise is this:

Close your eyes and breathe out three times. See yourself as a farmer preparing the ground to receive grain at the site of the illness. Breathe out once. See yourself now as a warrior. Catch and subdue a dragon. Remove all of its teeth. Plant these teeth in the furrows you have created around the illness. Cover them lightly with earth. Move to one side, and see spear tips emerge through the earth, then see the spear shafts and the plumed crests of the bronze helmets. The rest of the head emerges, and as their lips pass the level of the earth, they emit a bloodcurdling yell that weakens all the cancer cells. Then their full bodies emerge. These Sparti warriors are clad in bronze armor, carrying shields and spears and wearing golden swords in their belts. As they line up in rows, their faces are fierce and weather-beaten.

They now hunt the enemy cancer, destroying it completely, uprooting it and destroying it everywhere in your body. When they are finished, they then turn on each other. After they destroy themselves to the last man, see and sense how your body feels. Breathe out, and open your eyes.

This exercise can be done for one to two minutes three times a day: early morning upon rising, at five or six in the evening, and before bed. A seventy-two-year-old woman's lung cancer disappeared after she did this exercise three times a day for twenty-one days.

First Imagery Exercises

The following set of seven powerful imagery exercises were created from *The Egyptian Book of the Dead*, one of the most significant healing texts ever written. Its origins date back to 4000–5000 B.C.E. (Before the Common Era).[1] The first four are to be used for general healing. Do whichever exercise you choose once a day for twenty-one days for one to two minutes at a time. Don't use more than one exercise in any twenty-one-day period. Wait seven days before starting another exercise. The last three are used for specific purposes clearly stated.

 Name: **Serpent in the Sun**

Close your eyes and breathe out two times. See the serpent of illness entering the sun and being burned up. See him vomiting the evil he has made. See the Egyptian sun god, Ra, kissing the poison and turning it into magic. The serpent's vomit is turned to gold. (You do not need to know what Ra looks like. However you imagine him is fine.)

Breathe out one time, and let this golden light fill you inside and out, above and below, knowing that your illness is disappearing. Breathe out one more time, and open your eyes.

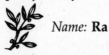 *Name:* **Ra**

Close your eyes and breathe out three times. See, feel, and sense yourself to be a swallow flying up the ladder of heaven. Sit in the hands of the Egyptian sun god Ra. He buries you in the blue egg of the world. Breathe out one time. Feel and sense yourself pressed into the soil. Now, begin rising, becoming a new person, growing toward the sun. Then breathe out, and open your eyes.

If you are religious, sit in God's hands rather than Ra's.

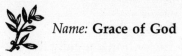 *Name:* **Grace of God**

Close your eyes and breathe out three times. See, sense, live, and feel the grace of God as three humming lyres.

Breathe out one time. See, sense, live, and feel the grace of God like a single thread that wraps itself around you, becoming the whole cloth of your being. Breathe out, and open your eyes.

 Name: **Sticks of Light**

Breathe out slowly one time as you close your eyes. See and sense the ten thousand sticks of light being raised against the darkness. Know that the demons have fled. Breathe out, and open your eyes.

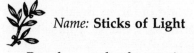 *Name:* **The Falcon of Gold**
Intention: For self-transformation
Frequency: In early morning and at twilight, for 21 days; 1 minute at a time

Close your eyes and breathe out three times. See, sense, and feel yourself being released from a blue egg as a falcon of gold and rising above the world. Breathe out one time. See yourself sailing on golden wings. Know what it is to live, to love, to know, to change, to embrace the infinite. Do not forget this becoming.

Breathe out, and open your eyes.

Name: **Becoming the Swallow**
Intention: An exercise for bringing faith to your-
      self
Frequency: In the early morning and at twilight,
      for 21 days; 1 minute at a time

Close your eyes and breathe out three times. See the dark marrow of your bones becoming light.

Breathe out three times. See yourself becoming the swallow flying above a world of forms. Breathe out one time. Now, becoming formless, make of yourself what you at first imagine.

Breathe out one time. Be the swallow passing between two worlds of sky and earth. Know what it is to believe.

Breathe out three times. Climb the ladder of heaven. Brush the stars with your wings, and fly straight to the heart of the universe. Return slowly and easily, landing lightly on the earth. Come back to your human form. Breathe out and open your eyes.

Name: **The Golden Flame**
Intention: For general health and well-being
Frequency: In the early morning and at bedtime,
      for 21 days; 1 minute at a time

Close your eyes and breathe out three times. See and know that you belong to no one unless the golden flame of a lamp. Breathe out one time. Know that this lamp, inaccessible to us, keeps our courage and silence awake.

Breathe out, and open your eyes.

More General Healing Exercises from Colette Aboulker-Muscat

Name: **Sea Rocks**

Intention: For seeing clearly; to give a gnosis, prognosis, and healing

Frequency: In the early morning and at twilight, for 21 days; up to 3 minutes at a time

Close your eyes and breathe out three times. See yourself *as* the sea at high tide—perfectly quiet, flat, shining, and full. Know that *as* this high tide, nothing may sever it or you. Breathe out one time. Look under the clear quiet surface, and see the steep strong rocks that are the potential or actual "mal-ease," disease or emotional difficulties, scars, or irritants. Breathe out one time. Sense and feel how when in full form and high as the tide, we are resisting them and are mastering the consequences of their presence. Breathe out one time. Recognize the source of them for what they are. But, to be sure of what they are, wait for the level of the tide to descend. Look at the ones you want to get rid of. Be sure to *breathe* and *concentrate* your energies. Be sure and do it! Be sure of succeeding. See the main rock of your disturbance disappearing by disintegrating into the tide that is rising and then going out. Breathe out, and open your eyes. Take 21 days to get rid of the main rock, recognizing it, looking at it, and sensing it.

Name: **De-armoring**

Intention: For relaxation and self-transformation

Frequency: Each morning for 21 days: 1–2 minutes at a time for week 1, 30–60 seconds at a time for week 2, and 15–30 seconds for week 3

Close your eyes and breathe out three times. See yourself standing before a gate wearing your suit of armor—the one you wear to protect yourself from the world. Breathe out one time, and begin removing this armor piece by piece, beginning with the helmet, putting all the pieces behind you, and seeing yourself naked. Breathe out one time. Open the gate, and go into the garden, closing the gate behind you. Find yourself in a luxuriant garden full of birds, flowers, and trees. Listen to the birds singing, and smell the fragrance of the flowers. See a clear pool in the center of the garden, and enter the clear, clean, crystal, cool water of the pool, and cleanse yourself thoroughly. Come out of the pool, then dive in once again, going to the bottom, where you find something of importance for you. Bring this up to the surface with you, and leave the pool; then find a brand-new set of clothes to put on. Afterward leave the garden by the gate, and when you are outside, breathe out and open your eyes.

Name: **The Agony and the Ecstasy**

Intention: For general healing

Frequency: Once a day for 21 days; 1–2 minutes at a time

Close your eyes and breathe out three times. Live and know what is life and death. Having lived them, try to know what they really are. Having known and lived life and death, cast out anger, guilt, anxiety, disease, and old age. Now burn them. Then burn the ashes. Note what you feel and know about burning ashes. Afterward, know that you can do anything. Then know that your hands are sky and earth. With these hands you are able to weave your own life. Know that you are able to weave your own life with the threads and colors you choose. See and recognize the working out of the pattern that your own weaving is starting. Breathe out, and open your eyes.

Name: **The Healing Journey**
Intention: For general healing and cleansing
Frequency: Once a day, for 7 days; 3 minutes at a time. This exercise may be repeated at the same time every year for a 7-day period

Close your eyes and breathe out three times. Find yourself on a beach at the base of a cliff. Know how you have gotten to the base of the cliff. Afterward, look at the white cliff, and with a sharp stone engrave all the distressing feelings that have been plaguing and bothering you. Engrave these traits deeply into the stone. Then lay out a white sail on the beach below the cliff. Take a hammer and chisel, and break up the traits. See the stones breaking up and falling from the cliff into the white sail. Gather them up in the white sail, and tie up the four corners of the sail to make a bag. Then gather together wood taken from shipwrecks at the bottom of the sea, and make a boat. Get in the boat, and start sailing from the shore where you are located. Go through waterways, meeting people of different countries and relating to them by adopting a response different from that habitual trait in the bag. Eventually, turn into the deepest part of the Pacific Ocean and drop the bag into it, seeing it disappear from view. Come back feeling lighter. Take the boat in the opposite direction, back through the Pacific, back through the waterways, stopping along the way to learn about the people and understanding them. Then come back to the shore from which you started. Now look at the fresh cliff and use a sharp piece of metal, if you need it, to remind yourself *not* to touch this freshness. Jump up now to the top of the cliff with your new lightness, and in a meadow there, let yourself be quiet and relax. Afterward, breathe out, and open your eyes.

Specific Healing Exercises

The following four exercises refer to specific conditions that a vast majority of people experience. If someone you know is experiencing them now, share the exercise with them or, with their permission, do the exercise for them as a process of "distant healing." Madame Muscat devised the first three, while I created the fourth.

Name: **Sand Salutation**
Intention: To relax
Frequency: In the early morning and at bedtime, for 21-day cycles, 7 days off between cycles; up to 3 minutes at a time

Close your eyes. Breathe out slowly three times, and see yourself stretched out on a beach. See the sun above you to the right. Feel the salutary heat and the radiant light envelop you, cover you, incubate you, and penetrate you. See yourself extending your arms toward the sun and catch the rays, bringing them back to the nerve center of your solar plexus (located about 2 inches below the lower end of your breastbone). Breathe out one time. Feel and see the rays spreading from your solar plexus, which becomes the radiant center of your entire organism. See and feel these rays becoming increasingly blue, like the blue light that surrounds the sun and lights up the sky and that now flows inside you like a long and calm river, spreading its vivifying light. Feel the entire organism stimulated by a rush of life, streaming full of tranquil and joyful force.

Name: **Seeing Tomorrow**

Intention: To get rid of a painful feeling or situation

Frequency: Each morning, for 21 days, or fewer if the difficulty is resolved before then; up to 1 minute at a time

Close your eyes. Breathe out three times. Imagine yourself *now* in the situation you are experiencing as painful. Then, see how you look in this situation one week from today; then one month from today; then one year from today. At each instance know that the current situation is in the past. Note what you sense and feel. Now breathe out, and open your eyes.

Name: **Be as a Tree**
Intention: To heal cancer
Frequency: In the early morning and at bedtime,
for 21 days; 20–30 seconds at a time. If you
do more 21-day cycles, take 7 days off between each

For a religious person: Close your eyes. Breathe out
slowly, and see your body as a tree shaken by the hand
of God. See and sense the dead bark stripping away
from the trunk, and all the insects falling to the ground
away from you. Breathe out, and open your eyes.

For a non-religious person: Close your eyes. Breathe
out slowly, and see your body as a tree shaken by a great
storm. See and sense the dead bark stripping away from
the trunk, and all the insects falling to the ground away
from you. Breathe out, and open your eyes.

Name: **From Servant to Sovereign**
Intention: To change the victim attitude
Frequency: Once a day, in the early morning, for
21 days; up to 3 minutes at a time

Close your eyes. Breathe out two times. See and
know what it means to be a "victim of circumstances."

Breathe out one time. Sense and know that the victim is you without will. See, sense, and know that without will we cannot create. Breathe out one time. Sense
and know that without creating, we are always the
"child of fate," everything seeming to happen by chance.
Breathe out one time. Know that with will, we can turn
chance to choice. Breathe out three times. See, sense, feel,
and know that choice is the child of will and the father
of freedom.

Breathe out one time. Sense and feel that to be without will is to be bewitched. Breathe out one time. Know this bewitchment.

Breathe out two times. As the victim without will, you are now under the spell of the wizard who is preparing you for the sacrifice.

Breathe out one time. Now evict those bewitching beings that are sapping your creativity. Be sure to conquer them. Breathe out one time. See and feel what it is to vanquish. Afterward, be convinced of this victory.

Breathe out one time. See yourself becoming famous, your name being spoken in a loud voice. Breathe out, and open your eyes.

I created the following exercises for the different anatomical/physiological systems: nervous, digestive, skeletal, urinary, respiratory, and circulatory. The exercises promote a healing for the system as a whole rather than one specific part of that system.

Name: **The Galaxy**
Intention: To cleanse and heal the nervous system
Frequency: Once a day, each morning on awakening, for 3 cycles of 21 days. In week 1 of each cycle, do the exercise for 1–2 minutes; in week 2 of each cycle, do it for 30–60 seconds; in week 3 of each cycle, do it for 15–30 seconds

Close your eyes and breathe out three times slowly. See, sense, and feel yourself reaching up to a new star in the galaxy. Bring down the energy of this star as a stream of white light to stimulate the astrocytes of your brain. (Those star cells contain the enzyme that stimu-

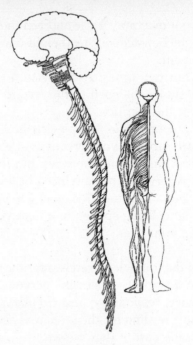

NERVOUS SYSTEM

lates the neurons to fire their electrochemical substance.)
Sense the astrocytes releasing their enzymes, which you
see as streams of yellow light blanketing all of the neurons and bringing them to life. See and sense the neurons giving off their blue electrical impulses, that you
sense and see moving rapidly down the nerve fibers like
the landing lights at an airport. These impulses flow to
the anterior horn cells of the spinal column and from
there, through the nerve fibers, flowing directly to the
muscles.

See and sense your muscles contracting and relaxing, sending a stream of red light back up the nerve
fibers, the flow moving in the reverse of the blue light

and reaching all the neurons in the brain. Note what happens. Breathe out slowly, and open your eyes.

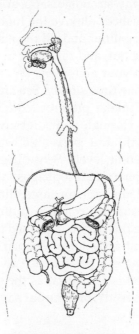

DIGESTIVE SYSTEM

Name: **Becoming the Snake**

Intention: To cleanse the digestive system

Frequency: Once a day upon awakening, for 21 days; 1–2 minutes at a time. This exercise can also be done for up to 1 minute a half hour before each meal

Close your eyes and breathe out three times. See yourself gently zipping open your abdominal cavity. Reach in, and remove the entire digestive tube. Turn it inside out and wash it in a cool, fast-flowing, fresh, clean mountain stream with a fine golden brush. See, sense, and feel the water rushing over the tube, washing away all the debris removed by the golden brush. See the debris as black or gray strands disappearing downstream. When you are finished, remove the tube from the water and let the sun dry it out and fill the entire cavity. Turn the tube right-side out, and replace it in your abdominal cavity and zip up your abdomen.

Breathe out one time slowly. See and sense yourself now as a snake. Take a piece of food, and swallow it. As the food goes through your digestive system, sense and feel the rhythmical peristaltic waves pushing it along at the different levels. Sense it going from your mouth into the pharynx, esophagus, stomach, duodenum, jejunum, ileum, cecum, ascending colon, transverse colon, descending colon, rectum, anus. See the fecal mass coming out perfectly formed as a solid golden cigar-shaped form that is buried deep in the earth. Know that the snake has the perfect digestive function, and that your digestion is as natural as the snake.

When you are ready, breathe out and open your eyes.

CADUCEUS

Name: **The Caduceus**

Intention: To straighten or elongate the skeletal
   system

Frequency: Each morning upon awakening; 1–2
   minutes at a time

Close your eyes and breathe out three times. See the
two snakes of the caduceus winding around your spinal
column, going from below upward to the top of the column. As they do, see, sense, and feel your spinal column
elongating, straightening, and taking on the shape of the
snake.

Breathe out three times slowly. See yourself binding
the bones of your back and neck with a sheet. Wind the
sheet tightly around yourself. See now the sun rising

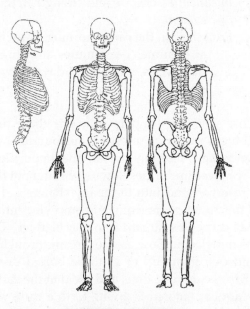

SKELETAL SYSTEM

over you as you rise on your two legs to see it. Know that this binding is so tight that you can walk steadily, your feet digging into the earth, your head tossed to the sky.

Breathe out one time. See your bones as if for the first time, knowing how they fit together. Fall in love with your bones. Hear your arms calling to your wrists and elbows, your legs calling to your ankles and knees. Hear the language your feet speak to your head and skull.

Breathe out three times. See, sense, and know your body as the book of all you remember, as the bones of the living God. When you are ready, open your eyes as you breathe out slowly.

Name: **The Reservoir of Health (1)**

Intention: To cleanse and strengthen the urinary system

Frequency: In the early morning, at twilight, and at bedtime; 1–2 minutes at a time; for 21-day cycles, stopping 7 days between each cycle

Close your eyes and breathe out three times. See your kidneys as a large reservoir, surrounded by a beautiful landscape, filtering out all the impurities of the body. See these impurities flowing throughout the layers of the reservoir and into the many channels at the bottom of this reservoir, meeting and emptying into the ureters that carry this stream into the bladder. There the streams mingle and flow as one stream through the urethra and out of the tip of it, to be buried deep in the earth. Breathe out one time, and see that the earth where the stream has entered is giving forth a fruit, vegetable, or flower. Know that as this fertilization takes place, the urinary tract has healed. Breathe out, and open your eyes.

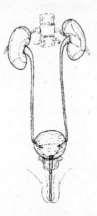

URINARY SYSTEM

or

Name: **The Reservoir of Health (2)**

Intention: To cleanse and strengthen the urinary system

Frequency: In the early morning, at twilight, and at bedtime; 1–2 minutes at a time; for 21-day cycles, stopping 7 days between each cycle

See, sense, and feel that your kidneys are a large reservoir that filters a vast volume of blood. See this filtering system in layers, each layer arrayed like grains of corn on a cob. Sense blood flowing through those layers, and sense the dissolved wastes being separated from the blood. The new purified blood returns upward through the large renal vein to the heart. Breathe out one time. See and sense the wastes flowing in two spiral currents. These currents are yellow, with black or gray strands moving through the ureters into the bladder where they meet to form one strong spiral current that eddies and empties into the urethra and flows through it and out its tip as a long arching stream, which disappears deep into the earth. At the same time experience the rhythmical upward movement of the blood into the heart, where it receives pure oxygen.

Breathe out, and open your eyes.

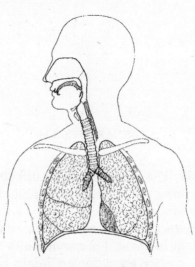

RESPIRATORY SYSTEM

Name: **The White Light**

Intention: To cleanse and heal the respiratory system

Frequency: If you are experiencing respiratory discomfort—once every hour or two while awake, up to 3 minutes at a time. If there is no respiratory problem—once in the early morning, for 21 days; 1–2 minutes at a time

Close your eyes and breathe out three times. Now inhale. See, sense, and feel white light enter through your nose and flowing into the bronchial tree. See the white light flowing through the larynx into the bronchii and from there filling your lungs. See your lungs expanding like a bellows, allowing the white light to enter. See and sense your chest expanding at the same time. As you exhale, see the bellows contracting forcibly, pushing out the impure air—now mixed with carbon dioxide—through your mouth and drifting away into the atmosphere as gray smoke, like cigarette smoke. At the same time, see and sense your chest contracting. Repeat this exercise twice more before opening your eyes, knowing that your respiratory tree is working rhythmically.

Name: **The Infinite Heart**
Intention: To regulate and cleanse the circulatory system

Frequency: If you have a circulatory disturbance—every hour, 1 minute at a time, for 21 days; for circulatory cleansing—in the early morning and at bedtime, for 21 days, 1 minute at a time

Close your eyes and breathe out three times. See, sense, and feel your vascular tree becoming like the sign of infinity (∞) with the heart at the center. Know that your circulation is moving infinitely as this infinity, never resting and circulating forever. See this circulation moving from red to blue, then blue to red, and find yourself becoming the rhythm of this eternal undulation. Know that this flow gives life to your entire body. Breathe out, and open your eyes.

CIRCULATORY SYSTEM

Turning to God

The following exercises are intended to help you make the turn to the invisible reality. Their theme is repentance, which means "turning again." Embodied in repentance, then, is a returning to God.

Madame Muscat furnished the first exercise; I take full responsibility for the second exercise, on the Ten Commandments.

Name: **Returning to Yourself, or Self-Remembering**

Intention: To stop habitual destructive behavior; to connect with the invisible reality

Frequency: Once in the early morning, for 21 days; the whole set for up to 3 minutes at a time

Close your eyes. Breathe out slowly one time. Know, live, and feel repentance as a universal phenomenon.

Breathe out one time. Know that repentance is the highest expression of man's capacity to choose freely.

Breathe out three times. See, live, and feel repentance as the extrication from the binding web of your life.

Breathe out two times. Sense and feel the relationship of repentance to time. Breathe out one time. See and experience changing time's significance to present and future.

Breathe out one time. See and know how by turning again, we are able to truly repent. Breathe out one time. See and know how, by turning we are truly repenting. Breathe out one time. See, know, and feel how repentance brings an answer only when we *really* turn from our errors.

Breathe out slowly, and open your eyes.

Name: **The Ten Commandments**
Intention: To know your moral nature
Frequency: Once in the early morning, for 21 days; up to 3 minutes at a time for the whole set

Close your eyes and breathe out three times.
1) Know and feel that there is no other god but God. Breathe out three times slowly.
2) Imagine yourself in the museum of your past personal life. See yourself breaking all the statues you have placed there and ripping up all the paintings that you have made. Breathe out three times.
3) Become a seed planted in the earth. Sense and

know your growing as this seed, and know
from where the nutrients come. Breathe out
three times.

4) See and live yourself walking backward
through the day. Note what you experience.
Breathe out three times.

5) See, feel, and know that your parents are *your*
creation. Be reborn in a new way. Breathe out
two times.

6) See and feel anger. Take one step back from it,
look at it again, and laugh. Breathe out one
time. Choose life. Be aware of what you are feeling. Breathe out three times.

7) Know how to separate the oil from the water.
Do not let them get mixed again. Breathe out
one time. See and know that when letting them
get mixed up, again we adulterate our own life
force. Breathe out three times.

8) See and know what is meant by the statement,
"To steal from others is to rob yourself of life.
To steal from yourself is to rob others of your
presence." Breathe out three times.

9) See, sense, and know that silence is golden.
Breathe out one time. See this silence becoming
golden. Breathe out one time. See this golden
silence encircling you. Become aware of what
you experience. Breathe out three times.

10) See yourself sitting at a sumptuous banquet table. You are with complete strangers. Breathe
out one time. Eat your meal, but begin each
course by giving away your portion to one of
the strangers. Note what you feel. Breathe out
one time, and open your eyes.

Awakening to Spirit

This next exercise group, supplied by Madame Muscat, opens the possibility of entering an awakening to spirit. Do one each day for 21 days, and wait 7 days before doing the next. The sequence is up to you.

Name: **Light**
Intention: To awaken to spirit
Frequency: Once a day in early morning; 1–2 minutes at a time

Close your eyes and breathe out three times. You are in a long narrow ancient Egyptian barque on the water in a dark tunnel. It is so dark that you can discern absolutely nothing. You hear the water around you lapping on the boat and the walls, and the oars in the water. Then, at the front of the boat you can begin to see the dim outline of a sail. It can barely be made out. You go to the front of the boat and find the sail that can be more clearly made out, flapping in the breeze. At the bottom of the sail, you find a ball that can be seen more clearly as more light begins to enter.

As the scene becomes clearer and clearer, you see that the ball is a golden one and that its light brightens all, and that the sail, attached to the mast, is a radiant and transparent one. Your body becomes the mast and is covered by this radiant transparent sail as you watch the sun rise *very slowly* in front of you. You find yourself, as you are watching the sun rising, begin to rise with the sun. You then remove the sail from the mast by lowering it, and then putting it around your shoulders as a white cape. Become aware of the sensations that happen and continue watching the sun rise.

Descend from the boat and come back to the chair,

opening your eyes and continuing to watch the sun rising, and describe the sensations to yourself.

Name: **The Victorious Wind**
Intention: To enter the life of spirit and make a
    turn toward it
Frequency: Once in the early morning, for 21
    days; 1–2 minutes at a time

Close your eyes and breathe out three times. See yourself in a vast, clear, quiet, verdant meadow. Sense the victorious wind moving the green grass. The meadow is full of flowers the wind is moving. Sense it on your skin. Look at the iridescent forest at the edge of the meadow. The trees are bending. Look at the river bordering your meadow. Look into the river from the meadow. Sense the electricity from the coils of currents running through the river. See yourself diving from the meadow into the convolutions of the water. Then, go into the translucent vastness of the river. Sense and see above you the verdant winding river waves. Breathe out four times. Be there underwater—and now *vault* up to the meadow. Hear the whispering mystery of the saying, sighing, swaying of the silvery forest. Breathe out one time. Looking up at the top and at the right, *enter* into the heavenly vacuum of the spirals of power of the electric coils flowing between the meadow and sky. Sense how these spirals are returning you to the void and from there back to the grassy vastness of the meadow. Breathe out, and open your eyes.

Name: **The Black Mirror**
Intention: To enter spiritual life
Frequency: Once in early morning, for 21 days;
    1–2 minutes at a time

Close your eyes and breathe out three times. Cautiously, look at each of your earthly limitations. Put each of them in the big bag of secrets. Breathe out one time. With a spade, dig a deep path carrying your bag, follow the passage you are tracing into the depths of the underworld. Go on until you reach the hidden black lake. Breathe out one time. Open your bag, and throw each limitation into the black water. Name each of them loudly, inwardly when you throw them away. Look at each limitation as it disappears into the black water. Breathe out one time. Then, look at yourself reflected into the black mirror of the hidden waters. Breathe out one time. Now that you have freed yourself of limitations, make your way back to the level of the earth. Breathe out between each new step and each new effort, and feel how as you are ascending that you are regaining freedom. Sense how this is your reintegration into your humanness and in reality makes you different. Breathe out one time. See how transcendence is happening when you find a break through obscurity and a return to clarity. See yourself becoming clear. Breathe out one time. Sense how this is coming from washing away the restrictive, frustrating limitations. Breathe out, and open your eyes.

Mirror Exercises

The mirror serves a unique function. As I mentioned in Chapter 2, looking into the mirror shows us the "whole picture," as it were. Put one hand up to a mirror. The reflection in the mirror you see is your other hand. Your hand has been reversed. The mirror has revealed the "whole picture" to you.

The reversed hands also define the meaning of analogy. Although the two hands have obvious likenesses, *they are not the same*. There are obvious differences and similarities between them. These two hands are analogous to each other, mirror reflections of each other. Moreover, the physical and nonphysical, the outer and the inner, are reflecting each other. Mirroring and analogizing are synonymous.

Mirrors are the dividing line between concrete reality and other levels of reality. The image reflected in the mirror is form without substance; it has *no* locatable reality in dimensional or measurable space. In practice, mirrors are nonjudgmental and unpolluted reversing devices that show us the opposite of our habitual views, free of our habitual responses to everyday life.

The power of the mirror to reflect inner life was shown by Oscar Wilde in *The Picture of Dorian Gray*, a novel in which the deteriorating character of the protagonist was reflected in his portrait, mirroring the changes in his inner life. Mirrors appear in other forms of literary expression as well. In the fairy tale "Snow White and the Seven Dwarfs," the witch-queen has a magic mirror that provides her with answers—and reassurances—most of the time. The classic example of mirror experience was provided by Lewis Carroll in the adventures of Alice on her journey through the looking-glass.

Imagery work may use mirrors in two ways. There

are imagery exercises that are to be done before a mirror, with eyes open. This type of exercise lasts roughly a minute and is used to obtain something in the present situation. Other imagery exercises involve imagining various experiences in a mirror, with eyes closed. This type of exercise is used for inner transformation or for bringing new opportunities. What follows are several exercises of each type.

Mirror Exercise with Eyes Open

Standing before a mirror and looking into it is useful to help achieve some immediate goal right now in your life, such as going for a job interview, meeting a date for the first time, delivering a speech to an audience, playing in a chess tournament, or any of a hundred other possibilities. For these exercises, simply use the bathroom mirror as you wash up in the morning.

Name: **Mirror Exercise with Open Eyes**
Intention: To obtain something
Frequency: Once each morning before the intended event

First imagine a white circle around the mirror. Know it is there so that you don't have to maintain that image. Then look at yourself in the mirror and say the first sentence of whatever is relevant to the situation. For example, if you are interviewing for a new job, you might say, "Hello! My name is Bill Smith, and I am pleased to meet you." The articulation of the words should be *slow, exaggerated,* and *very clear.* Pay particular attention to your lips enunciating the words. At the same time, see alongside your face an image of whatever it is that you are seeking, such as, Bill Smith getting the job. As soon as you complete the sentence, see the white circle open. The exercise is to last no longer than articulation of the sentence. Remember, don't be concerned about the outcome.

Mirror Exercises with Eyes Closed

There are numerous therapeutic applications of mirrors with eyes closed, including the single-faced mirror, the double-faced mirror, and the triple-faced mirror.

Single-Faced Mirror Exercises
The single-faced mirror shows your face now, its present truth. In this mirror you find images that are constructive or destructive. You can perpetuate the inner meaning of the constructive images by imagining yourself standing before the mirror and with your *right hand* wiping away the image in the mirror from *left to right*. This activity has the effect of putting that image into the future, since movement to the right means future and transformation. Conversely, you can remove the impact of disturbing images by imagining yourself before the mirror and pushing the image away, out of the mirror, from *right to left* with your *left hand*. This movement to the left pushes things away into the past.

The single-faced mirror can be used in many other ways. Here are some examples:

Name: **Single-Faced Mirror Exercise (1)**
Intention: To resolve disquieting feelings
Frequency: Twice a day, in the early morning and at twilight, for 21 days; 15–30 seconds at a time

Close your eyes. Breathe out three times, counting backward from three to one. At one, breathe out once more and see the one becoming a zero. See the zero growing in size a bit and becoming a circular mirror. Looking into the mirror *see* and *resolve* lacks and limitations. Breathe out once, and wipe the image away to the right, with your right hand. Now in the blank mirror, see and resolve *repression* and *frustration;* then *envy* and *acquisitiveness;* then *insecurity* and *uncertainty;* then *doubt* and *hesitation;* then *hostility.* Wipe the image away to the right each time. After you finish, breathe out and open your eyes.

Name: **Single-Faced Mirror Exercise (2)**
Intention: To correct painful memories
Frequency: Each morning, for 21 days; 30–60 seconds at a time

You can use the single-faced mirror to look at the past, see events, and experience the feelings happening then.

Close your eyes, and breathe out slowly two times.

At those ages, see yourself resolving a painful situation. Wipe the situation away to the right with your right hand. Then breathe out one time, and open your eyes.

Name: **Single-Faced Mirror Exercise (3)**
Intention: To find a direction in life or make a
    decision
Frequency: Once as needed in each situation

Close your eyes and breathe out three times. Into
the mirror find a path leading to a door at the upper
right. On the door see a sign stating the purpose of the
exercise, such as "the door of decision," or "my career
choice." Enter through the door, close it behind you, and
see what you find. Afterward, return through the door,
down the path, and out of the mirror. See yourself standing in front of the mirror, seeing what you have discovered in the mirror, and wiping it away to the right. Now
breathe out, seeing the mirror disappear, and open your
eyes.

Two-Faced Mirror Exercises
While the one-faced mirror exercises are essentially
connected with purifying yourself, the two-faced mirror
gives you the opportunity to see a future possibility.
Naturally what you discover in the mirror, you must
carry out in your daily life.
The two-faced mirror is excellent for healing both
emotional and physical disturbances. Here are two examples.

Name: **Two-Faced Mirror Exercise (1)**
Intention: To correct something
Frequency: As needed, whenever it comes to
    your attention

Close your eyes and breathe out one time slowly.
Into the mirror see the image of a trait, quality, or phys-

ical aspect of yourself that you don't like or find deficient in yourself. Then turn the mirror over quickly, and see in the other face the aspect corrected. See how you look. Wipe the image away to the right with your right hand. Then see the mirror disappearing, and open your eyes.

The following exercise is for people who are indecisive.

Name: **Two-Faced Mirror Exercise (2)**
Intention: To act or make a decision
Frequency: Once a day, for 21 days

Close your eyes and breathe out one time slowly. See yourself between two mirrors. In the left mirror, see and feel yourself to be a mummy, experiencing all the feelings of being a mummy. Catch the end of the bandage lying over the navel and unwrap it. Make the bandage into a ball, and throw the ball into the center of a large dark cloud that has formed in the blue sky above you. See the cloud breaking up, releasing its stored rain, washing over you and cleansing you. Breathe out one time. In the right mirror, see yourself singing, dancing, and happy. Then wipe that image away to the right with your right hand. See the mirrors disappear, breathe out, and open your eyes.

Three-Faced Mirror Exercises
The three-faced mirror presents you with the possibility of transformation, allowing you to look at what was, is, and will be. Here, *will be* refers to your intention about a future possibility. You imagine a three-faced mirror before you: One face is to your left, one to the center, one to your right.

Name: **Three-Faced Mirror Exercise**

Intention: To make a change in your life or find a new direction

Frequency: Once, whenever you feel a change should be made, or when you need to find a new direction

Close your eyes and breathe out three times. In the mirror at the left, see what was; in the center, see what is now; and in the right, see a future possibility. After you look to the left, wipe the image away to the left with your left hand. Then breathe out one time, and look in the center mirror. If the image there is painful, wipe it away to the left with your left hand; if it is a useful image, wipe it away to the right with your right hand. Breathe out once more, and go to the right mirror. Wipe this image away to the right with your right hand. Then breathe out once more, and open your eyes as the mirrors disappear.

Spiral Exercises

The spiral represents the movement of life itself. In embryological development, the morula and blastula unfold in a spiral movement. The Milky Way galaxy moves in a spiral manner. Other examples of spirals are tornados, snail shells, and DNA structure. Spiral movement combines the vertical and horizontal movements and is the culminating form for movement. Since the spiral denotes the movement of freedom, we can move out of our space-time dimensionality for a brief moment through it. Since the spiral also represents growth, it gives the meaning of creativity. The spiral is the symbol not only of creation but of birth and decreation, matter and spirit, renewal and decay, and generation and decomposition in everyday life. Finally, the spiral also means finding the best in ourselves, the rhythm of our life.

We can use spirals either imaginally or concretely. Concretely, we draw them. In imagery, for the treatment of phobias, compulsions, and sexual disturbances we use spirals to rid ourselves of old habits. For depression, we use spirals to energize ourselves. For physical ailments such as arthritis or muscle spasm, we use the movement of spirals to massage the muscles and cleanse the bones (see page 162–3).

Name: **The Spiral of Many Colors**
Intention: To get rid of a sexual problem (impotency, frigidity), compulsion or phobia
Frequency: Once a day, for 21 days, or less if the disturbance is eliminated before then

Close your eyes and imagine yourself drawing a spiral in concentric circles clockwise, starting from the inside and going outward. Draw this spiral in color, starting at the center. Use the color you most dislike there, and go to less-liked colors and then to the ones that you like. From there go to the ones that you most like, and end with your favorite color, which goes out to the right like an arrow. It looks like this:

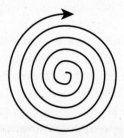

Then, draw this same spiral physically on a sheet of blank white paper.

This next exercise uses physical activity rather than imagery to lift depression associated with loss of energy and motivation:

Name: **The Spiral of Energy**
Intention: To give yourself energy
Frequency: Each morning, as needed; 2–3 minutes at a time

On a drawing pad, use a pencil to draw spirals from inside, going out, in a clockwise direction—as in the drawing—any number of times. Keep focused on your intention while you make the spirals.

Life Plan Exercise

In the twelfth century the prominent physician and teacher Maimonides wrote a very influential book called *The Guide to the Perplexed.* In this book he spoke of how we can overcome disturbing traits by invoking the opposite tendency, thereby creating a balance in ourselves. Maimonides was speaking essentially of the union of opposites, a method described in the earliest spiritual traditions all over the world as a way of inner development.

The union of opposites is a mental act of will that impels us toward acting or thinking in a nonhabitual way. In mind medicine, this process is called Life Plan and was developed by Muriel Lasry-Lancri, in Paris. In the Life Plan you take any number of characteristics and convert them to their opposite through an act of will.

The characteristics can be any distressing emotional or physical traits that are creating your suffering. You find out what opposite quality these can change to by simply closing your eyes and asking yourself what opposite characteristic would emerge if that tendency were to be cut off. In doing so, you receive an answer that comes as a sensation, feeling, image, or word. You can then replace the trait with its opposite by remembering to change the trait to its opposite every time you become aware that the trait is present.

A color that connects the two traits can serve as a reminder of our intention to make this change. When you become aware of the trait, *stop* for a moment and acknowledge it, close your eyes, and in your mind's eye see the name of the tendency. From right to left see the colored line go across to a central point and from there to its opposite, seen as a word. Then open your eyes. It is as simple as that—the whole process takes just a few seconds. Do it every time you become aware of the disturbing trait coming up in your daily life experience for twenty-one days. On day one we give ourselves the intention that we are going to change [name of trait] to [name of opposite tendency], and the reminder to us will be the color [name of color]. Work with only one characteristic at a time for each twenty-one-day period.

As you do the Life Plan, you may find that the opposite tendency comes to you not as a word but as an image, sensation, or feeling. If that should happen, it is fine. Eventually, you may experience the characteristic and quickly see or sense its opposite even without the colored line. Also, if you should forget to use your will and lapse into the habitual trait, then later on when you remember that you forgot to use the Life Plan, stop at that moment and do the Life Plan.

As an example, take the trait of anxiety. Let us say

that its opposite is balance. You spontaneously find a color that links them—say, blue. On day one, you say that you are going to change anxiety to balance, and your reminder will be the color blue. Then, when you become aware of anxiety in your life, you *stop* for an instant and close your eyes. You see the word *anxiety*, and the blue line coming from that word to the center point and going across to its opposite, *balance*. At that moment, you say the word *balance* silently, then open your eyes.

At the end of twenty-one days, stop the Life Plan for seven days. At the end of the seven days, assess whether you have imprinted the new quality. If you have, choose another characteristic and begin work anew. If, at the end of the seven days, you decide that the imprinting has not taken, then continue to work on that trait for two more cycles of twenty-one days on and seven days off.

Stopping Exercises

A major element for training the will is what I call "stopping." Our education and habituation trains us to immerse ourselves in experience. When we experience frustration or pain, mental or physical, we want relief from it. We usually jump into experience to find that relief. Multitudinous temptations urge us to experience some gratification that will supposedly lead us to happiness: "If that experience didn't bring the happiness you expected, don't worry—the next one will." On and on, this faulty education misleads us. The serpent coaxed Eve to experience by eating the apple: Through it, she would achieve happiness and immortality. She had the choice to *stop* and listen to the voice of God but did not take it. The rest is history—our history. Given the choice of stopping, watching, and listening—or diving into experience—we generally choose the latter.

Stopping habituation and giving new direction to the will is in itself an act of will. Stopping reflexive activities and placing the will under conscious control is an act of healing.

Stopping exercises are a reversing technique to break habits. These exercises are simple to do, and although they require the shortest amount of time to do, their effects can be profound with practice. The principle is to alter momentarily the rhythm of a habitual activity, or to delay a particular emotional pattern of reactivity that causes difficulty.

Such stopping provides a short shock to the system, which stimulates the body to respond in a new way while waking you up mentally. The range of these exercises is: 1) stopping a habitual activity momentarily (like not turning on a light switch); 2) giving something up that you love or is meaningful to you, for a brief time (like coffee for a 24-hour period); 3) cleaning a small space for a minute or two each morning for 21 days with the intention of cleansing yourself; 4) reversing the events of the day in your mind before going to sleep at night.

Among the innumerable ordinary daily activities that you can stop, begin with those with which you have the strongest connection or from which you would like to gain the most distance. Pick only one element to work on in any given three-week period. Some of the common activities include:

1) making a telephone call
2) answering the telephone
3) smoking a cigarette
4) eating

5) turning on a light switch
6) turning a doorknob

Each stopping exercise has an intention. If you wish to stop smoking, you would hesitate for an instant and recall your intention—by saying "no smoking" or seeing yourself throwing away the cigarette—before you remove the match from the box, or before you strike the match, or as you place the match at the end of the cigarette. The stopping action lasts for only an instant. Whether you complete the action or not is up to you.

In making a telephone call, as you bring your finger to the dial, stop this action for just an instant. In that instant, say the intention of the exercise, or see an image representing your intention. For example, "patience" might be your intention. As you stop for an instant before dialing, say "patience" to yourself. Whatever follows is accepted without judgment. With eating, you make a stop as you bring the fork or spoon to your mouth.

Stopping is an ongoing practice that requires that you remember to do it consistently for twenty-one days, then stop for seven days. If you feel your intention requires more work, then resume the stopping exercise for another two cycles. Otherwise, move on to a new one.

If, during the course of practicing stopping, you should forget to carry it out, don't berate or criticize yourself. Simply accept this fact and carry on with your practice, but start the twenty-one-day cycle over, since your rhythm has been interrupted.

Decreation Exercises

Decreation is a technique of will that uses imagery to remove unwanted beliefs from consciousness. This technique has a long history; for example, it has been an integral part of Tibetan Buddhist practice for centuries, as is described in the Tibetan Lama Tartang Tulku's book, *The Hidden Mind of Freedom*.[2] The field of Western mental imagery has long known that disturbing images—beliefs—are to be removed from consciousness.

In the twentieth century, the psychical-spiritual Theosophical movement published important works that indicated that all movements of mind—be they impulses, feelings, images, or cognitive thoughts—become mental forms, or thought forms, with shape and dimensionality but without substance, volume, or mass.

These mental forms are the analogue of physical forms and are translated into physical activity. These mental forms, our creations, are like our mental children. Once birthed, they assume a life of their own and exert influence, as our physical children exert influence over us. We do their bidding, just as we tend, nurture, and feed children. *Once created*, objects in the external world, as well as inner objects like mental forms, can have power over us.

For all practical purposes, all mind events are mental forms and are beliefs given form. Since our beliefs are what we can actually control in our lives, we can create and decreate them at will and thereby make a huge difference in our lives.

First, get used to the fact that every sense perception, physical symptom, and emotional experience you have is at first a belief. See your disturbing image—or word, if an image doesn't materialize for you—on a blackboard. With an eraser, erase the image from the blackboard to the left with your left hand. In place of the erased image, see a new image or word that signifies a life-choosing direction. This exercise is to be done in the early morning and at twilight for up to twenty-one days. One person erased the disturbing word, and the word *life* appeared in the center of the board. After repeating this process, he experienced a significantly beneficial change in his attitude toward life.

Chanting

Chanting is another way to change habitual tendencies. Cultures throughout the world have long used it to quiet the mind and establish a new vibratory harmonic. Chanting is a form of music, and the healing effect of music has long been known, even in biblical times when David played the lyre to soothe Saul's melancholic state. Ulysses' men were seduced to their deaths by the sirens' singing. In the Western traditions, chanting is utilized in Jewish services, in Gregorian chants, and in Islamic Zikr services.

Although the effects of chanting have not been thoroughly studied through quantitative measurement, they have certainly been described by people who have experienced them. Everyone knows that music can produce "altered states"; that sounds can affect muscle tone and increase energy levels has been amply studied by Dr. John Diamond.[3]

Our chanting exercise utilizes the Western musical scale and the pitches mi-do-re (E, C, and D of the C major scale). The words to be chanted are all three syllables long, and they are of three kinds: *key, bell,* and *need. Key words* are used to open or unlock something within. *Bell words* are used to produce or promote balance, harmony, or resonance. *Need words* are used to change a habit. Any chanted word, regardless of the group it belongs to, acts as a natural tranquillizer or antidepressant. A starter list of these words is shown in

Key Words to unlock something within	Bell Words to promote harmony or balance	Need Words to change a habit
Mercy*	Emotion	Energy
Fortitude	Foundation	Mazaltov
Bravery	Energy	Completion
Competence	Harmony	Lioness
Courageous	Balance*	Synthesis
Expansion	Fulfillment	Direction
Stamina	Amen*	Calm*
Repentance	Shalom*	Patience*
Openness	Unity	Centeredness
Clarity	Freedom*	Temperance
Awaken	Wisdom*	
Sacrifice	Intention	
Attention	Renewal	
Awareness	Mandala	
Endurance	Becoming	
	Proportion	

the chart above. Ultimately, you can amass your own set of words that best fit your particular situation.

Begin by standing up straight, relaxing, closing your eyes, and drawing in a deep breath. Sound the word as you breathe out; take another breath if you need it. The word is to be pronounced in a particular way: The first syllable is short and distinct; the second is sounded for an extended period and is distinctly pronounced; with the third, the movements of the mouth exaggerate the pronunciation until it disappears musically and ends as an exaggerated but distinct sound.

Let us say that you are feeling confused and foggy and have decided to chant the word *clarity*. Separate the word into three distinct syllables: CLA-RI-TY.

First syllable:	CLA is chanted to the "mi" sound and is short and distinct.
Second syllable:	RI is chanted to the "do" sound and is sounded for an extended period, distinctly pronounced.
Third syllable:	TEE is chanted to the "re" sound and is exaggerated.

Let yourself move into the word as you chant it. Enter and become the word, with no active thought.

You may notice that certain two-syllable words are also amenable to a three-note mi-do-re intonation. Several of them appear on the list, denoted with an asterisk.

Chanting exercises are to be done for twenty-one days. Chant the word three times in the morning as you begin the day, and three times in the evening before you retire. Each chanting session should last no longer than one and a half minutes. On the first day of the cycle, tell yourself your *intention* or what you wish to obtain through the chanting. For example, you might say, "I am doing this chanting cycle in order to gain competence." You would then chant the word *competence* for three weeks, stop for seven days, and then begin another cycle with a new word.

Prayer

As imagination is thinking with God and contemplation is resting with God, so prayer is speaking with God. Prayer is an inner supplication that is recited either silently or vocally, calling upon the invisible reality for help. Any form of call upon the invisible reality may be considered prayer. For instance, mental imagery is concretized prayer. Along these lines, Dr. Randolph Byrd studied the positive therapeutic effects of prayer on patients suffering from coronary heart disease.[4] He found that those who were prayed for had significantly lower severity scores, based on the hospital course after admission. They required less ventilatory assistance, antibiotics, and diuretics than the control group.

Prayer is most effective in enhancing our lives when it is nondirective—that is, when we do not ask for a direct outcome. Praying to God to "heal my cancer" or "have me win the lottery" is to be avoided. Direct prayer of this type usually fails, leaving us feeling bitter and disappointed in God. Direct prayer does not work precisely because it is invested in outcomes. Concern about the outcome sets the stage for it not to happen. A direct prayer has the effect of attaching us to the outcome rather than to God.

A corollary of this point is the commonly reported paradox: "When I gave up all hope of what I wanted ever happening, that's when it happened." Giving up all hope means giving up all *false hope*, that is, thoughts about the future, achieving an outcome, or gaining future rewards. Hope for the future is *always* false hope, since it puts our attention onto the outcome. As soon as we let go of our hold on the future, we often receive an answer that satisfies exactly what we had wanted.

So prayer has to be nondirective. This means that

we ask for help in bringing our own will into alignment so that we can achieve something. For example: "Please give me the strength and courage to fight my illness." Or: "Please show me the way to find an answer for what troubles me." These prayers are aimed at finding direction, not achieving a result. In the Gospel of Matthew, as we have seen, it is written: "Seek and you will find, ask and you will be answered, knock and the door *will be* opened"—we do not open it; it is opened for us. All of our prayers are built around this dictum.

A miracle is something new in our lives, or something that has brought something new into our lives. A miracle occurs without precedent, without our experiencing it before, either individually or collectively. Nevertheless, miracles do not happen out of nothing. They are an alchemical process of changing something that is already there into something else. They are events in the invisible reality that have effects in the visible reality. The parting of the Red Sea happened at the Red Sea. Moses struck a rock with a staff, and water came out— the rock was already there. Jesus turned water into wine—water was already there. Prayer is a catalyst for these miraculous occurrences.

Prayer cannot be a deal offered to the invisible reality: "I'll be a good guy *if* you do this for me." There are no deals with the Divine. We ask, seek, and knock, and the answers come. But we must take the first step. We have to show our trust in the invisible before, not after the fact. Make the necessary changes first, then see what happens.

There is a moral component to prayer. If something in a prayer is morally misaligned with the commandments, the prayer cannot be answered. The invisible reality cannot participate in a morally impure act. This is not to deny that people have prayed and enlisted dark forces to aid them. But the price paid for such activity affects not only the individual but the people around him or her, who might come under the sway of that demon. I have Hitler and Stalin in mind here.

One of the most beneficial results in my clinical work comes when I introduce the existence of angels. Angelology is a central theme in all three major Western religious traditions. There are 109 references to angels in the Old Testament and 174 in the New Testament. The Islamic tradition has a vast angelology. Medieval and Renaissance Christian art depicts a flourishing of angels. Early Catholicism taught the existence of the guardian angel. It is an ancient idea that we are each born with at least one guardian angel who is present to help us *whenever it is summoned*. This last phrase is vital. A guardian angel cannot come if we do not summon it. Philo, the first-century Hellenistic Jewish philosopher and mystic, said it succinctly: "Make no mistake, angels are real." I have personally experienced my guardian angel, as I attested in my opening remarks in this book.

Angels (and demons) are a reality. They are beings of the invisible world that surrounds us. We really have to get used to the fact that the invisible world is a reality that affects us. There is a constant interplay between the visible world of our experiences, events, and behavior and the invisible world of imagination, dreams, beliefs, and beings.

If we live in a virtuous manner, we have easier access to the realm of angels, whom we may call upon to help us. These angels are congenial and are waiting to serve and help us in every way possible. They are emissaries of the divine being. Guardian angels do not participate directly in human affairs unless they are summoned.

I have witnessed many people asking of their angel and being answered, including the clinical situation. The angel must be summoned actively; otherwise it remains in a state of twilight sleep, a torpor that is a tragedy for the angel. The angel must be called upon.

Close your eyes, and see a cloud of maternal green presence over your head. Ask then of your guardian angel for whatever it is you want. Have no qualms or hesitancy about asking. There is nothing too trivial or extravagant to ask for help with. Remember that if it is not morally correct, however, it cannot be accomplished. Also, do not be concerned with the outcome. Often I experience an indication that something has happened within twenty-four to seventy-two hours. The guardian angel never stands between us and God. Rather, it acts as an escort who will take us toward the divine.

I have found that we usually call on God when we have a critical need, either for ourselves or someone we care about. We call on the guardian angel when we have a personal emotional need for help in some immediate situation in everyday life.

These prayers can be used for general healing through mental imagery; they have come from the creative wellspring of Madame Muscat, who adapted them from holy scriptures:

1) Close your eyes and breathe out three times. Regard yourself as a shining flame burning brightly without name and form. Know and see how the complete meeting with the infinite is eternally within ourselves.

2) Close your eyes and breathe out three times. By listening to the silence, hear the life in yourself being the helper of your life. Breathe out one time, and see and hear the life in yourself being the helper of all life.

3) Close your eyes and breathe out three times. See and know by looking at the window of the inside that you are the guardian of yourself. Breathe out

one time, and see, feel, and know by watching at
the outside that you are the guardian of your
brothers.

4) Close your eyes and breathe out three times. Feel
and know that you stand *really* in front of your Creator. Hear that the Creator is *really* answering you.

Do each of these prayers each morning for seven
days. Begin week one with prayer 1, week two with
prayer 2, week three with prayer 3, week four with
prayer 4.

Exercises for Resurrection

The final exercises in this chapter are the momentous climax to which mind medicine brings us. These
two exercises for resurrection were devised by Madame
Muscat and myself, respectively.

Name: **Awakening Osiris**
Intention: To resurrect
Frequency: Once a year on the same day in the
early morning; up to 3 minutes at a time

Osiris, murdered by his brother Seth, was cut up
into fourteen pieces. Each piece was buried by Seth in a
different part of Egypt.

Close your eyes and breathe out three times. As Isis,
Osiris' wife and the goddess of wisdom, you have to recollect the fourteen pieces. See yourself searching for the
bones until you experience finding them all. Gather them
together, and make the spinal column. Take a magnetic
chain made by the hands of two people and place it behind
the neck at the level of the cervical vertebra to awaken the
dead. As you do this, say "SA" (which means life, the hi-

eroglyph (𝄞), giving life again. See, feel, and sense what happens. Breathe out one time. Then find a vase of clear water, and pour it over Osiris, saying inwardly "KRI" (which means movement). Then say inwardly "SHMS" (meaning Go!), resurrecting Osiris to eternal life. Breathe out three times. Now that you have resurrected the dead, you must bathe and cleanse yourself in the Lake of Mystery. See yourself swimming south within the canal within the lake, and emerge at the end of the lake. See a scarab beetle (see illustration), and say inwardly "SHH" (meaning resurrection and re-creation), seeing your new creations forming from now until eternity.

Name: **Turning Back the Hands of Time**
Intention: To resurrect
Frequency: Once a week at bedtime, on your
           sabbath; 1 minute at a time

Close your eyes, and breathe out three times. See before you a clock with the second and hour hands set at the time you are doing the exercise. Now, breathe out one time slowly, and turn the hands of the clock back to any inner or outer event that distressed you at that time. Correct that experience, and when you are finished, turn the hands forward to the present time. Sense and know that your physiology and emotions have harmonized. Breathe out, and open your eyes.

9

Resurrection: Healing Into Immortality

Death, thou shalt die.

—JOHN DONNE
"Death Be Not Proud"

This chapter brings us to resurrection, the culmination of mind medicine. Traditionally, Judaism, Christianity, and Islam have defined resurrection as the restoration of the dead souls to life as a *literal* fact. However, there is another resurrective understanding that these great religious traditions have not emphasized but that has been a focal point of Western spiritual traditions: Death is not inevitable and can be overcome. That is, *we can put an end to death.*

To my readers who are not spiritually inclined, the possibility of endless life may seem incredible. But the possibility of life extension is neither incomprehensible nor irrational—nor is it out of reach. On a recent TV show on longevity, scientists said in the not-too-distant future, human beings can be genetically engineered to live for *200,000 to 300,000 years*. At first, I couldn't believe that modern scientists were talking soberly and seriously about immortality as a physical reality. Yet life extension is considered a real possibility. What I have offered in this book is how to achieve life extension using the mind.

For my readers who are spiritually inclined, overcoming death has special meaning. The body is usually understood as a temporary house for an invisible guest called the soul. The soul is inhabiting the physical casing on earth to learn lessons so it can make its way back to God, from Whom it has been severed. In the Jewish mystical tradition (and later in Christian mysticism), the spheres of physical and spiritual life are one—that is, body and spirit are infinitely connected. Body, mind, spirit become joined in an harmonious trinity, making union with God. The body as well as the soul or spirit is immortal. We are not meant to die. Instead of dying, we may develop a *resurrective body*, one of freedom, love, light, and a *different physiology* that is indestructible, as the scientists I mentioned envisioned.

When we act out of love or hate, truth or falsity, morality or immorality, our biology and physiology clearly undergo a profound concomitant shift. Much evidence for this fact has been accumulated in recent decades. A compelling study done at Harvard University by psychologist David McClelland shows this biomental moral relationship. In his experiment, Dr. McClelland showed a group of forty Harvard students a film of violence. Before doing so, he measured an immune fraction taken from the inside of their cheeks. The immune fraction he measured was IgA (immune globin A). When the students were shown the film of violence, this IgA fraction went down. He then showed them a film of Mother Teresa. Afterward, about half the students said that she was a phony or a charlatan. Yet despite their comments, that half as well as the rest of the sample showed an elevation in the IgA fraction.

In another study, at Mount Sinai Hospital in New York City, a reasonably large sample of about thirty recent widows and widowers were examined for their immune functioning. Those who were clearly depressed about the death of their mate showed a notable decrease in immune functioning. In fact, so accurate were these measurements that monitoring the levels of immune functioning over a period of months, the investigators could predict which individuals would not recover from their mourning and who very well might die quickly. Those whose immune functioning did not return toward normal after several months were considered at high risk for disease and death. The prediction turned out to be accurate. A study at another medical institution discovered that smiling showed a correlative increase in immune functioning, while frowning showed a corresponding decrease in immune functioning.

The movement toward resurrection, then, involves not only a social, emotional, and spiritual turn but a shift in our physiology, with an accompanying surge of lightness. These shifts, I believe, will become increasingly more possible and will eventually be realized when the trinity of truth, love, and morality descends onto this earth. The advent of this trinity can allow us to create a "resurrection body," encompassing our physical, emotional, social, and spiritual lives, as we turn away from the will to power to the will to love. In our resurrection bodies our physical and spiritual nature join because our lives are dedicated to truth and our hearts dedicated to love. Our hearts allow the fulfillment of the divine commandments on earth and bring the possibility of God's light to shine through us.

God offered us immortality based on recognizing that we are made in His image and likeness, bearing the immortal seed of God (the image) and the moral virtue of God (the likeness). The image and likeness bear an indissoluble connection to each other.

Immortality, through perpetuating the immortal seed manifesting in us, clearly depends on our becoming God's likeness, becoming morally virtuous. The world is a moral creation of God, which we have been given the task of preserving but that we also have the possibility of destroying. When we attain the likeness of God and become morally virtuous, we shall become immortal. This task is everyone's to accept or deny, but it is *the* essential task of all of us. The fundamental problem in human life thus replicates the problem Adam and Eve encountered in the Garden. Each of us faces the same moral dilemma and must come to some decision about it.

The serpent promised immortality to Eve if she ate from the Tree of Knowledge. By usurping the place of God, like God we too may become immortal. The aim of medicine and natural science is to find the means to attain longevity and immortality through the processes devised by the serpent—that is, control and domination over the "future." Medicine tries to achieve immortality by curing all disease on earth. Natural science attempts to discover the laws and operations of nature, allowing us to gain dominance over it and thereby providing the means for attaining longevity.

In my opinion, these goals cannot work, as they depend on circumstances beyond our control, such as knowing and controlling the outcome of events. By using our will, imagination, and memory to effect a change of mind and heart, by bringing together mind and body in a blending of intuition and love in the service of truth, we just might fulfill the prophecy of ending death, as ancient sages envisioned thirty to forty centuries ago.

The idea that death can be overcome implies eliminating a standard about death as "bad." People may think, "Look how terrible it must be that I have to die and have not succeeded in living forever," or, "I must be a failure at this mind medicine stuff because I got sick and I'm not supposed to."

The techniques of mind medicine help us understand how to *ask* for resurrection. We cannot resurrect. That possibility can only be granted from the realm of spirit—from God. However, we can ask, seek, and knock—in other words, make the request. In mind medicine we can link our individual will with divine will, creating a shift in consciousness. The three elements that make this possible are truth, love, and morality.

Healing begins and ends with truth. Illness is an outgrowth of untruth, and the movement from illness to wellness is the correction of untruth and becoming true to ourselves. The basic task of life is to seek after truth, the shortest route to finding God. God has given us images and glyphs by which we can discover who we really are and what we need to do to correct our errors; the Ten Commandments to allow us to act morally in accord with divine truth; and resurrection, the possibility to live in the image and likeness of God as immortal beings by replacing the will to power with the will to love.

It is not difficult to discern what is false in life.

When we are living in the past or the future, or when we are not living in harmony with the Ten Commandments, we are not living the truth.

The most widely held false belief is that we shall become old, diseased, and eventually die. It seems absolutely preposterous, even impermissible, to consider a contrary belief because almost all our past experience shows that death is inevitable. I say "almost" since the Bible recounts that Enoch and Elijah did not die.

In the Western religious and spiritual traditions, death is not regarded as an absolute fact. Death can be overcome. It is *not* to be accepted as the natural or normal outcome of life. This was what ancient wisdom meant when it spoke of resurrection.

Resurrection means that the dead will be restored to life, or that those living will not die or may experience a rebirth while still alive. In the Bible, the prophet Elisha helped to bring a dead boy back to life. In the Book of Ezekiel the prophet, the dead are brought back to life in the valley of the bones. Other prophets talk of the days of the Messiah, when the dead will rise and come back to life. The Book of Daniel speaks of those days when there will be no death. Jesus demonstrated the possibility of resurrection, first by recalling Lazarus from the dead and then by coming back to life himself after he was murdered by the Romans. To emphasize the importance of resurrection, Maimonides—perhaps the most influential thinker on Jewish life since the Middle Ages—said that one could not consider himself a Jew if he did not believe in resurrection. Every Jew attending synagogue anywhere in the morning prayer service repeats this statement. A current thinker, Rabbi Adin Steinsaltz, one of the most influential spokesmen on modern Jewish thought, wrote recently:

The basic attitude of Judaism to death, which, it is said, was ushered in with Adam's expulsion from the Garden of Eden, is that it is not a natural, inevitable phenomenon. Death is life diseased, distorted, perverted, diverted from the flow of holiness, which is identified with life. . . .The world's worst defect is seen to be death. . . .The remedy is faith in the resurrection. Ultimately, "death and evil"—and the one is tantamount to the other—are dismissed as ephemeral. They are not part of the true essence of the world. . . .

In the combat of life against death, of being against nonbeing, Judaism manifests disbelief in the persistence of death, and maintains that it is a temporary obstacle that can and will be overcome. One sage, prophesying a world in which there will be no more death, wrote: "We are getting closer and closer to a world in which we shall be able to vanquish death, in which we shall be above and beyond death."[1]

The Western tradition has always asserted that the means for immortality are directly at hand, in and as our own individual being, and that by our applying these means, God shall heal us of our afflictions, both emotional and physical. Acts of self-remembering restore us to life, as Isis restored Osiris. Through life-restoring acts, we achieve immortal life.

Science and religion, medicine and healing, meet in the spirit of the path to resurrection. Religion means being tied to God. It is the science of the inner life. The original doctors were priests as well, and the original healers were prophets. The prophetic tradition of the

Jews points us toward the possibility of returning to the paradisiacal nondisturbed state of Eden.

The Jewish people announced the idea that all human beings might be destined to become prophetic men and women, evolved beings who communicate directly with God. The prophetic theme was taken up by Christianity in the person of Jesus, and by Islam in the person of Mohammed.

It is this vision of prophetic man that provides the inspiration for resurrection medicine. Prophetic men and women start out as ordinary human beings who suffer, make mistakes, become ill, and use ordinary human experiences to take stock of their lives and launch themselves on a new journey in life to return, like the prodigal son, to their *true* home.

I discovered the stages of our individual moral evolution in the book *The Vision and the Way* by Jacob Agus,[2] in which he described the "ladder of virtue" with the chart on the next page.

Resurrection carries some conditions for us to fulfill. It is not simply given to us—it has to be earned. Even though, like enlightenment, resurrection is a possibility for us, it is not a right to which we are entitled. We do have to change our consciousness and move from the will to power, domination, acquisition, and egocentrism to the will to love, cooperation, sharing, and selflessness. Such a shift in consciousness heralds the age of messianism. This age reveals either a messiah, a being disseminating knowledge, or knowledge itself that is disseminated by many who have had firsthand experience of the glory and promise of the will to love.

The messiah is someone, or a group of someones, who show the *way* to this knowledge. They are *never* our saviors. Each of us has to save ourselves so that we get off the endless cycle of destruction, death, and rebirth.

the study of wisdom literature
(the great religious and spiritual writers)

↓

alertness (remembering)

↓

alacrity (cheerful willingness)

↓

stopping of immoral activities
(following the Ten Commandments)

↓

purity (cleansing)

↓

piety (devotion/faith)

↓

humility (awakening)

↓

refusal to sin (correcting of errors)

↓

holiness (wholeness)

↓

holy spirit (love)

↓

resurrection

In the West, we do so by plunging into this sick world and curing both it and ourselves. We make our own Golden Age. None of the messiahs who have appeared in history have meant themselves to be a savior. They have been guides who show the way. It is the only legitimate job for a messiah.

To be shown the way, and to find salvation through that way, necessitates an individual will. Every so often, God sends us emissaries who try to show us the mistakes we are making. He cannot do more than show.

Each of us has a choice as to what to do with this knowledge. Choice always rests in our hands, as does free will.

None of the great messianic personages—Moses, Jesus, Buddha, Krishna—heralded or instituted a messianic age, a golden age of truth, love, peace, and harmony. The messianic age is yet to come, a glorious golden age to be experienced here on earth. In this evolving age, in which we are now on the threshold, there will be resurrection, eventuating in the end of death and disease as we know them. There will be a union of human will with divine will, and experiences en masse of illumination and union. In recorded history this has never happened before.

Endless methods are available today to permit us to remember ourselves—this is the easy part. The hard part is to become interested in finding our way back to the Edenic existence and to sustain the motivation to do so. The pull and lure of the material world is tremendous.

Each one of us is called to take the Edenic path by giving up our attachment to materialist notions and our overweening interest in things. And that is the rub! No matter how many techniques are at hand—and a great many are, in our land—they are of limited worth unless a concomitant value system values them. I have seen people falter in seeking meaning in life because they have not understood the importance of having a value system that treasures giving things up. One must take a vow of poverty and reject the riches of this world, instead of becoming a "spiritual materialist" who tries to grab spiritual life through the acquisition of material goods and deceives himself into believing he is leading a spiritual life. Spiritual materialism underlies the current popular interest in trance mediums and psychic channels who tell you your future for a sizable fee while promoting the virtues of prosperity and acquisitiveness.

Here spiritual tenets are shaped to fit in with the prevailing materialist desires, in order to rationalize them. Yet there is no genuine spiritual system I know of where impoverishing ourselves is not a prerequisite for restoring ourselves to Eden.

Resurrection implies that we become able to overcome terrestrial gravity—that is, all that pulls us down—and be pulled *upward* by celestial gravity. The force for achieving this ability is the vital constructive force, which was called in ancient days *zoë* (pronounced "ZOH-ee"). *Zoë* is a Greek term for life force. The other Greek term is *bios*. *Zoë* is life-giving life, while *bios* is derived life. In spiritual medicine there is a life force that is God, runs the universe, and permeates our planetary existence. It is a vertical force coming from above, down into our physical plane or world. This force is called *zoë*. The stars channel this force from other galaxies, universes, and levels of reality, down to ours. It is the source energy—analogous, I suppose, to the *chi* energy described in Oriental medicine.

Bios is the derived energy flowing from the source and energizing the sentient beings of the animal and vegetable, kingdoms that are living presences on our planet. *Bios* flows from generation to generation across hereditary streams in the human ecosystem. It is the vitality issuing from the vivifying source (*zoë*) and is the force of biological life. Other energy, for instance electricity, is not vital. It does not preserve life but depends for its creation on something dying. The same can be said for any form of combustible energy: steam, nuclear, oil, or gas. The force of *zoë*, on the other hand, is vital *and* preserves life; it is vivifying or life-giving.

The pull away from terrestrial gravity and toward celestial gravity heralds the shift in our attention away from the Tree of Knowledge of Good and Evil and to-

ward the Tree of Life. East of Eden, the cherubim guard
the Tree of Life. No one can look upon this tree and live.
The cherubim wield flashing swords to blind anyone
who dares approach. This protection is for our benefit.
We are not ready to see what this tree looked like. During the course of my own inner work, I had a flash of
what this tree looked like. It looks so:

It is *upside down*. The Tree of the Knowledge of Good
and Evil looks so:

It is *right side up*. This revelation from above filled me
with boundless hope and inexpressible joy. Governed by
celestial gravity, the roots of this tree are upward while
the branches are down—in a *reversal* of ordinary perception. The roots are nourished from above, from the invisible reality, from *zoë*. Life means that we are to reverse
our tendencies on the physical, emotional, social, and

moral levels. To choose life is to reverse the choice Adam
and Eve made in Eden. Life means that we are nourished
from above, that we are inextricably bound to the invisible reality for the perpetuation of our lives.

The first eight chapters of this book have explicated
the techniques that lead to the reversal of our ordinary
perceptions and to the resurrective possibility. These
steps are subsumed under the umbrellas of *remembering*
and *awakening*. We must first work against forgetting
ourselves and our indebtedness to the invisible reality,
against forgetting that we are our own authority, and
against surrendering ourselves as slaves to some outside
authority. The opposite of such forgetting is remembering. Remembrance is embodied in the archetypal story
of Osiris and Isis, as described in Chapter 7. Putting ourselves back together physically and mentally—literally
re-membering ourselves—is the major first step. With
remembering comes a restoration to life by awakening
out of the sleep, the hypnosis that we have allowed to
overtake us. When we remember and become awake, we
open ourselves to the resurrective possibility as a call
from above, rather than to the call from below known
as "death." We can choose to be pulled down by terrestrial gravity—the one that natural science is always trying to overcome—or to be pulled up by celestial gravity.
We can choose to die or to live. As God put it in ever
so many ways: "Choose Me, and live!"

Three dichotomies serve to orient us to this relationship. These three dichotomies are:

Forgetting—Remembering

Sleep—Awakening

Death—Resurrection

Forgetting is a partial sleep of the conscious mind,

in which some mental contents disappear. Sleep itself is the complete forgetting of sense perceptions and actions. In sleep, sense perception continues but at another level of reality, called the sleeping life. Death is a forgetting or sleep that involves our whole being—consciousness plus bodily functions. In death, we disappear fully from sense perception and the bodily world. The states of forgetting, sleep, and death are degrees of cessation.[3] The therapeutic thrust of spiritual medicine is to bring us out of the darkness of forgetting, sleep, and death into the light of remembering, awakening, and resurrection.

Remembering is a partial awakening of the conscious mind, while awakening from sleep is a remembrance of consciousness as a whole. Resurrection is the total awakening of bodily, soul, and spirit consciousness, lived as constant remembrance and experienced as total freedom.

For those of us who believe in reincarnation, I need to clarify the distinction between this phenomenon and resurrection. Reincarnation is the return to earthly life of the soul, which incarnates successively in physical form. Through successive births, the soul is able to overcome the trials of earthly life by mastering the earthly constraints of suffering, sickness, and death. For this opportunity to be presented to us again and again is an act of grace. In reincarnation, our physical being will never appear again on this earth; it is our bodily encapsulated soul that comes back. Our physical being as we know it disappears at death and will *never* reappear again. Reincarnation gives us a lengthened period to shoulder the pains of life that we have created for ourselves. The consequences we create for ourselves are our *karma*, an East Indian term that has become an integral part of the English vocabulary. It means essentially that for every act that we take, there is a consequence that we must pay.

This consequence may be beneficial or painful, but it is inescapable in the human life. *Karma* also means that for every action there *has* to be a reaction, which comes back to us either from the world or from ourselves, as in feelings of guilt.

Resurrection, on the other hand, is an alchemical practice of transmuting evil into good, constraint into freedom, sleeping into waking, death into life. It is an overcoming of death in which we reappear free of the constraints of suffering, sickness, and death, and without creating *karma* for ourselves. It is the final victory over sickness and death, the opportunity to free the world from its enslavement to sickness and death. Resurrection negates the need for reincarnation.

What does the resurrective possibility hold for future generations? Mind medicine can be taught to children so that they are not bound compulsively to repeat the errors of their ancestors. Their education comprises several elements, all of which can be practically taught: (1) the moral precepts, actively demonstrated to show how they apply in life situations; (2) the understanding that belief creates experience and the decreation of beliefs; (3) the value and practice of imagination as a useful way to understand that belief creates experience; (4) the practice of getting to the nondisturbed state through sacrifice rather than acquiring. The climate that will prevail with these teachings is love.

With truth, love, and morality as the pillars upon which spiritual medicine is built, what may come to be is what I call the age of resurrective medicine. Through communications, such as this book, we may be given access to the means to create substantial changes in our world, shifting it from a hostile and threatening one to a welcoming and embracing one. Throughout this book, I have presented contexts, methods, and techniques by which we are able to take charge of our lives. The crucial factor in changing our world is that our inner reality creates our outer reality: The invisible creates the visible. By utilizing mind medicine techniques, we may erode false mass-conscious beliefs and make our own personal reality healthy, happy, creative, and productive. Each of us who is participating in creating a new reality for ourselves can build a new belief collectively. The new collective belief that characterizes the resurrective age echoes words that the poet John Donne wrote several hundred years ago: "Death, thou shalt die."

Appendix

The chart on the next page represents a summation of this book. The Periodic Table of Western Spiritual Life and Western Spiritual Medicine lays out all the essential ingredients of mind medicine.

The Periodic Table of Western Spiritual Life and Western Spiritual Medicine

12 Techniques	3 Cornerstones	4 Memories	3 Logics	4 Mirrors
Imagination	Will	Factual	Quantitative	Inner–Outer
Will	Imagination	Logical	Functional	Above–Below
Memory	Memory	Moral	Qualitative	Before–After
Stopping		Vertical		Past–Future
Reversing				
Life Plan		**3 Vows**	**3 Dichotomies**	**6 Games (tricks)**
Chanting		Obedience	Forgetting—Remembering	Theology
Decreating		Poverty	Sleeping–Awaking	Government
Thinking by analogy		Chastity	Death–Resurrection	Medical Arts
Self-watching				Big business
Ten Commandments				Science
Prayer				

12 False Beliefs	6 Limiting Actions	Chain of Disintegration
The purpose of living is to be nondisturbed and gain pleasure while avoiding pain	Complaining	Expectations
We must gain approval	Sticking up for rights	Disappointment
We must get attention	Blaming	Hurt
We must be important	Trying to be different	Blame
Experience creates belief	Pleasing others	Disturbing emotional states: guilt, anger, fear, anxiety, or their derivatives
Gravity only pulls us down	Doing what authorities say	
Form gives rise to function		Physical symptom and/or addictive craving within one to seventy-two hours
There is chance		
Death is inevitable		
Truth and reality are the same	7 Keys to Healing	
We must be accepted	Sacrifice	
Outside authorities know more about us than we know	Pain	
	Quieting	
	Cleansing	
	Reversing	
	Forgiveness	
	Faith	

The following four acronyms cover the essentials of the Western spiritual medical model. They read across horizontally and are a convenient pneumonic to help remember them.

L	I	V
C	L	M
V	I	M
D	E	D

1.

L	I	V (e)	
Love	Inner calm	Value system	= Self-healing ingredients

2.

C (a)	L	M	
Cleansing	Light	Movement	= Key elements for imagery work

3.

V	I	M	
Voluntary will	Imagination	Memory	= Mind remedies

4.

D	E	D	
Doubt	Expectation	Denial	= Illness creators

The Periodic Table and the four acronyms are the unique contribution that I have been given to share with everyone. These two devices contain all the reminders we may ever need to find the road to self-healing and transformation.

May this contribution be the bridge between us to our eternal connection.

Love and amen.

Notes

Chapter 1: Mind Medicine

1. *Advances: The Journal of Mind-Body Health*, vol. 9, no. 4 (fall 1993).

Chapter 2: The Mirrored Universe

1. I am indebted to my good friend and colleague Dr. Francis Clifton for alerting me to this distinction.

2. I am grateful to Harry Palmer, an educational psychologist and founder of the "Avatar" process for expanding consciousness, who crystallized this understanding for me.

3. I must give Bob Gibson credit here for bringing to my attention some profound implications of this urge to attain the nondisturbed state. A now-departed friend, Michael Hampton-Cain, knew of my work on imagination and gave me a manuscript by his teacher, Bob Gibson, whose work has been instrumental in enlarging my understanding.

Chapter 3: The Moral Shield

1. I came across the phrase "unintended consequences of our actions" from David Bohm, a renowned physicist at Birkbeck College in England. The late Professor Bohm had been a student of Albert Einstein and of J. Krishnamurti, the noted East Indian teacher.

2. This trio of characteristics was formulated by Dr. Bob Gibson.

3. For an excellent in-depth discussion of the health and disease patterns that climbed to an all-time high in the 1980s, I recommend Leonard Sagan, *The Health of Nations* (New York: Basic Books, 1987).

Chapter 5: The Healing Relationship

1. I am indebted to Dr. Bob Gibson for the insight that symptoms represent natural adaptational responses.

2. I do believe, though, that it is necessary to quarantine people with infectious diseases so as not to endanger the larger community.

3. I am grateful to Leslie Meredith for furnishing this elegant way of understanding the lesson of Job.

Chapter 6: Why We Become Ill

1. Christopher Bird, *The Trial and Persecution of Gaston Naessens* (Berkeley: H&J Kramer, 1991).

2. These steps in the genesis of illness have been worked out by Dr. Bob Gibson.

Chapter 7: How We Become Well

1. Those interested in Waking Dream might write to me at P. O. Box 150, Gracie Sq. Sta., NY, NY 10028, about personal work training, and education in this area, which takes place under the auspices of my New York State Regents–chartered school, the American Institute for Mental Imagery (AIMI).

Chapter 8: Becoming Your Own Healer

1. I used the 1988 translation by Normandi Ellis called *Awakening Osiris* (Grand Rapids, MI: Phanes Press, 1988).

2. Tartang Tulku, *The Hidden Mind of Freedom* (Berkeley: Dharma, 1981).

3. Dr. John Diamond, *Behavioral Kinesiology* (San Francisco: Harper, 1979).

4. Randolph C. Byrd, M.D. "Positive Therapeutic Effects of Intercessory Prayer in a Coronary Care Unit Population," *Southern Medical Journal*, vol. 81, no. 7 (July 1988), pp. 826–29. The study was done over a ten-month period with 192 patients in the prayer group and 201 in the control group.

Chapter 9: Resurrection

1. Adin Steinsaltz, *The Strife of the Spirit* (Northvale, NJ: Jason Aronson, 1988) pp. 194–95.

2. Jacob Agus, *The Vision and the Way* (New York: Frederick Ungar, 1966).

3. This understanding comes from Valentin Tomberg, whose two seminal books are worth perusing: *Meditations on the Tarot* (Rockport, MA: Element Books, 1991), and *Covenant of the Heart* (Rockport, MA: Element Books, 1992).

Index

_____

About the Author

GERALD EPSTEIN, M.D., is in private practice in New York City, and is assistant clinical professor of psychiatry at New York's Mt. Sinai Medical Center. Dr. Epstein has more than twenty-five years of training in the mind and has been a pioneer in the use of mental imagery for treating physical and emotional problems. He is a leading exponent of the Western spiritual tradition and its application to healing and therapeutics. He has written many books and articles on imagery including *Healing Visualizations: Creating Health Through Imagery* (Bantam: 1989) and *Waking Dream Therapy: Dream Process As Imagination* (ACMI Press: 1992).

Dr. Epstein has lectured and taught worldwide. He is the director of the American Institute for Mental Imagery (AIMI), a postgraduate training center in imagination for licensed mental health professionals. He offers intensive weekend workshops in the use of mental imagery, open to all health professionals through the American Center for Mental Imagery (ACMI). In addition, he gives courses and group imagery for the general public.

Most recently, he is a recipient of a National Institute of Health Grant in Alternative Medicine to research the effects of mental imagery in the treatment of bronchial asthma.

Dr. Epstein can be reached at (212) 988-7750.